CW01590624

Laura Bannerman is a writer, holistic counsellor and personal development enthusiast who works with young women in self-connection and life design. She is driven to create accessible personal development tools for women so that they may connect with their inner voice and have the courage to embrace all that life has to offer. Laura currently lives on the Gold Coast, Australia.

Dedication

To the women who are ready to live.

Laura Bannerman

GIRL SEEKS LIFE: A GUIDE TO UNDERSTANDING YOURSELF

AUSTIN MACAULEY PUBLISHERS™
LONDON • CAMBRIDGE • NEW YORK • SHARJAH

Copyright © Laura Bannerman (2018)

The right of Laura Bannerman to be identified as author of this work has been asserted by her in accordance with section 77 and 78 of the Copyright, Designs and Patents Act 1988.

All rights reserved. No part of this publication may be reproduced, stored in a retrieval system, or transmitted in any form or by any means, electronic, mechanical, photocopying, recording, or otherwise, without the prior permission of the publishers.

Any person who commits any unauthorised act in relation to this publication may be liable to criminal prosecution and civil claims for damages.

A CIP catalogue record for this title is available from the British Library.

ISBN 9781788231312 (Paperback)
ISBN 9781788231329 (E-Book)

www.austinmacauley.com

First Published (2018)
Austin Macauley Publishers Ltd.
25 Canada Square
Canary Wharf
London
E14 5LQ

Acknowledgements

Thanks to Mitch, whose positive attitude and wholehearted support got me through moments of crippling self-doubt.

Thank you my parents who gave me the freedom to figure things out for myself. Thank you to all the strong women in my life – my mother, my sisters and my girlfriends. A special mention to my grandmother, Myrel – I hope I can be even a fraction of the strong, kind-hearted, open-minded and grateful woman that you are.

Thank you to Andrew Jobling, for helping me to believe that my voice was valuable.

Finally, thank you to every awkward moment, every painful experience, every kick to my confidence and every idiotic decision – my choices have created my path and my path has brought me to where I needed to be, every time.

Introduction

Mark Twain said, “The two most important days of your life are the day you are born and the day you find out why.” Ever since I was a young girl, I felt I had some kind of purpose to discover. I have always felt connected to something deep and spiritual, not that I could’ve articulated it back then. I dreamt of being a gypsy psychic, a fairy, a spiritual medium, a crystal healer, all before I was seven years old. The possibility of doing something magical felt real to me. I probably seemed very smug and weird to my two sisters. I like to think I was endearing to my parents, but this is debatable.

This feeling continued through my early years where I lived in a world of my own. Predictably, I’m a middle child and definitely had the syndrome. I played mostly on my own while my older sister, Brigit, bossed around her puppy – my younger sister, Julia. Anyone who has an older sister would understand, playing alone was almost always preferable and definitely less dangerous. If I did play with Brigit, she would change the rules in order to win and it seemed that every ‘harmless’ game would somehow end with me being tricked into eating soap.

So I spent many hours alone, dreaming of fairy colonies in ancient forests and how big my crystal ball would need to be in order to accurately predict the future. I begged my parents to take me to the markets and second-hand book shops where I pored over every title, hoping to come across a dusty, ancient spell book. I longed to understand the secrets of magic. I was sure I had special powers and just needed to find the resources to help me tap into them.

This might sound like I was self-assured and outgoing, but conversely, I was quite a needy, shy and anxious child, which forced me to be perceptive to other people's personalities and opinions. I was sensitive and impressionable so my weird interests didn't stick around for long once I realised they weren't 'normal'. Even if I thought that I might have special gifts, the world (my parents, teachers and friends) wasn't that interested. I learned to act in a way that ensured the most favourable response from others.

Don't get me wrong, it was all part of the growing-up process. No one forced me to stop using my imagination, though no one actively encouraged my daydreams either. Nonetheless, I've led a fortunate life; the same happy, reliable and mundane story of most people I know. Raised in an upper-middle-class family, it was reinforced from a young age that our family certainly wasn't on the bottom of the pile but we had to work for what we had. I was sent to a co-ed state primary school and then a private girls' high school. There were some hardships and family drama along the way. Some really stupid decisions thrown in for good measure. I did everything required of me, to some extent. I played the part as I was meant to, bratty teenage years included.

As I came out of my teenage years and into the Real World, I was hideously unprepared for the emptiness and loneliness I felt. To be fair, I really had nothing to complain about. I had a solid foundation and a supportive family. I was raised to be a quick, independent thinker and have an excellent work ethic. As soon as I was able to leave home, I got my licence and moved out. Peace at last! Or so I thought. Instead I felt lost. This was life? I felt a bit angry and cheated, knowing something important was missing.

I told myself I was fine, wiped the sweat off my upper lip and kept going, too stubborn to admit defeat. I hated being given advice and was so headstrong that I never really listened to anyone, wanting to figure it all out for myself. But I had also stopped listening to myself and remained a blind fish in a dark cave, swimming aimlessly from end to end – working, eating, boozing and basically living from day to day, surviving from week to week.

My insides melted with insecurity and jealousy of other people and their seemingly effortless lives. I aligned myself with friends that had experienced worse upbringings or had even needier personalities than me so that I could help them, save them even – in turn putting my own needs last so I didn't have to think about anything real. Eventually, I resented everybody around me because I'd made friendships based on my undivided attention on other people's needs. The thick walls I'd built around my internal void were impenetrable.

I had no idea where to begin fixing the mess I'd made. Secretly I wanted someone to just *get* me but without going through the process of really letting them in. I had a nasty combination of trust issues and low opinion of myself. I think maybe I was waiting for someone a bit cooler and cleverer to swoop in and take over. You know, transform my life for me. I certainly had no idea what I wanted.

These miserable patterns were painful to experience and I couldn't see the role that I was playing in my own demise. I was the victim and people just kept hurting me and doing the wrong thing by me. I ignored anything too painful and focused on working and building my professional career. I thought, "At least when I'm rich, I'll be able to figure it all out. When I'm rich, I'll know what I want. When I'm rich, life will be easier and I will be free." All the while, I continued to tread water and fight off psychopathic thoughts.

Hello, inevitable melt down… But, why? I did everything I was told, everything I was supposed to do. At the time, I felt alone and isolated in my experiences but as I got older, I learned that my feelings were common. Apparently, everyone feels like shit at this time of life. Well, I'm not okay with that!

My vision is to disrupt this status quo. Fast forward ten-ish years and I'm in a position where I feel compelled to chime in and do something about this.

I am now a qualified counsellor and my passion is personal development, from the practical day-to-day stuff right down to the soul level. I work with young women who have no idea who they are, what they want or where they are headed. I help them to rebuild their connection with themselves, using the tools I discovered the hard way and developed over years of trial and error. These are not lessons that we learn in school. These skills may be acquired as we trudge slowly forward in the adult world but why wait until we are thirty-plus to figure this stuff out? I want to help you recognise where you are going wrong and ensure you build a life you love.

I'm guessing you may be struggling with some big life questions, if you are reading this book. I bet you are strong, sensitive, smart and motivated. Maybe you just need a positive push forward or the seed of an idea planted in order to make your next move. Hopefully, this book will help you do that. It may not have all of the answers but it can be a place to start finding some of the right questions to ask yourself.

It wasn't an easy decision for me to put this book out there. I think back to the cringe-worthy poetry I wrote as a teenager and pray that I've developed my writing skills since then. God, how deeply I used to feel things. But, when I wasn't bleeding my way through verse, I would delve into someone else's story – books have always been my lifeline. If things were ever confusing or complicated (whose childhood wasn't?), I could always trust a book to provide me with an escape. Not just a distraction, a book could help me understand the world in words that I could never put together myself.

A great author makes you pay attention and gives you the gift of being able to simultaneously learn about the world and about yourself through reading a story that is not your own but validates your personal thoughts, feelings, dreams and fears. I hope that you can feel heard by reading this story because I know that I am not alone in my experiences. The resistance, the *stuckness* that you're feeling right now – I felt it too. It is the sign that you want more from life, but you're scared. You fear the changes that are necessary to become a fully-functioning human. And so, you've put your life on hold, waiting for the right time or the right opportunity – the thing that will save you from yourself.

My feelings about growing up were valid and yours are too. The purpose of this book is to put in print my own thoughts about how to be an Adult without experiencing complete self-destruction as you fight against the person that you are because of the preconceived idea in your head about the person you should be. This is my opportunity to communicate to you the total waste that it is to expect nothing more from life than the mainstream path we are conditioned to follow.

My message – you get to decide your life for yourself.

When we are children, we are allowed to be special. We are allowed to be ourselves. And then we start to reach a point, maybe between six and ten years old, depending on how militant your parents and teachers were, where we are expected to grow up, fit in with our peers and complete our schoolwork. The days are over of exploring that essence of who we are. We become a cog in the family unit, whatever that might look like, and life is the wheel that just keeps spinning.

Everybody's version of 'normal' is different. But for most of us, there is a common theme. We seek to fulfil certain needs, like love, security and significance. As we age, the ways in which we fulfil these needs change. When we are eighteen, we think our dream is to be rich, famous and powerful – to *be someone*. But what we really want is to be special, to be loved, and to be free.

I'm not saying that it is wrong to want to be rich and powerful – you can still have that. But let's peel back the layers of the onion to get to the core of that. By fulfilling your own needs of feeling secure, loved and special, you can be free now. It doesn't have to be the elusive and unattainable that make you happy. It's easier to become successful when you already feel successful and the path to financial success becomes a whole lot more enjoyable.

Coming to these conclusions and subsequently writing this book meant really getting to know myself. It has been an interesting process, digging through a lot of memories, unearthing a lot of negative beliefs and thoughts about myself. It has been painful and deep, but also positive and insightful, at times manically bouncing between emotions. Looking inward is scary but rewarding and empowering. I have revived confidence in myself.

Self-discovery is a journey – this might be the beginning of your path, or perhaps you are already well on your way. I've spent my early adult years relearning who I really am, which has been the most important process of my life so far. We all follow this process differently. Hopefully, you will stay with me to learn about my process and I hope that it has something to offer you.

TRUTH: You can have everything you want just by getting to know who you really are.

On the surface, it might seem simplistic, but how can you know what you want if you don't know who you are? Why wander through life collecting things and memories and experiences if you aren't going to create any meaning? You don't need a million dollars so that you can be free. You can be free now. You can be successful now. You can be happy now. You can be *you*.

At this point, you might be thinking that it all sounds like hard work. That actually, you're fiiiiiiiiiiiine. Well, I thought I was fine too. Until I looked around at the life I had built for myself in my mid-twenties and realised it was the opposite of what I wanted. And I had pushed away everyone who wanted to help me because I felt defensive. I was committed to staying with a partner that really wanted completely different things out of life. My friendships were shallow. I was anxious and depressed – I bordered on mentally ill, in fact.

Looking back, there were a lot of largely joyless years from the end of high school to moving out of home at eighteen and creating a life for myself into my mid to late-twenties. Sure, I'd had some fun times but the recurring low points were confusing, lonely, empty, indulgent and sad. Instead of the freedom of trying new things and taking chances, in order to learn what I loved and what I wanted, I spent ten years contained within four secure padded walls of my own making. I did not yet have the flexibility or emotional maturity that I needed to look inside myself and figure out what I needed. And, God, I was stubborn.

Luckily, I woke up to myself and had plenty of time to turn my life around. For me, the process of making positive changes took me many long years. It was a trial and error mess that cost me a fair amount of dignity and thousands of dollars due to some expensive mistakes. Much of the heartache might have been avoided if I had just taken a LONG, HARD LOOK AT MYSELF. So maybe this book will catch you in freefall before you shatter. Or maybe it will help you pick up the pieces.

I want you to be able to feel empowered and inspired so that you can fulfil your dreams, whatever they may be. You don't even need to know what they are yet. The beauty of dreams is that they can be fluid and evolving as you move forward. Let my story spark your desire to realise your own story and potential. My hope is that you are able to overcome fear and self-doubt, gain more control of your life, learn to express and accept yourself, become free to grow and welcome change, be open to new chapters in life, release old beliefs, learn what it means to be a strong woman and navigate the balance of success.

Throughout each chapter, there are some reflections that may help you to apply my ideas to your own life. These can be valuable if you like setting goals or you want to map your thoughts as you read. But, if you're not the kind of person who enjoys their reading with a side of homework, you can continue reading without feeling like you are missing a crucial step. They will always be there to come back to if you choose. The most important thing is keeping an open mind to what is possible.

The real magic all begins and ends with you.

Chapter One
Emerging from the Chrysalis

Looking back...

When I think back to my teenage years, I recall two distinctly opposing flavours of experience. Firstly, the sweetness of daily hangs with friends, laughter, eating rubbish from the school tuck-shop, the pungent smell of Impulse and Lynx deodorant, weekends and school holidays at the beach, supervised and unsupervised parties, drinking for the first time, spluttering with the drag of my first cigarette, the awkwardness and thrill of becoming mates with boys, the bus to and from school and the melting pot of friends from different schools, first kisses – first everything. Becoming an object of desire and feeling significant to somebody else. The highs were dizzyingly high.

Then there were the lows which left more of a sour taste in my mouth. Feeling isolated and disconnected, friendships marred with backstabbing and bitchy comments. Putting others down and in turn being put down by others. Rejection from boys who seemed at the time to be the definite love of my life, not feeling pretty or cool enough. Shame and guilt after certain experiences. So many secrets. Loneliness and distrust. Having deep feelings and thoughts but being surrounded by shallow people. Wanting to rise above the bullshit but not having the emotional maturity to do it with dignity.

Our idea of our own self-worth and level of confidence correlates directly with how we're able to cope with the confusion during this time. Like most teenagers, I didn't have a particularly high opinion of myself. My strength was relative to whatever catastrophe was occurring in my social existence. I based my self-image on what others seemed to think of me, putting it out of my own control and in the hands of those around me. Depending on the day, I would feel good or completely wretched. For instance, the day that a boy I liked held hands with me after school, I felt pretty *spesh*...but the next day, when I was left out of a private joke during class, I felt ugly and unpopular.

There are so many words to describe those days. Self-centred, Narcissistic, alienated. Disillusioned, difficult, painfully secretive. Weird, wilful and wild. Both shameless and shameful, memorable and forgettable. Unbalanced, contradictory, complicated and full of muddy truth.

How on earth did we survive it? Looking back it feels almost predatory in nature, like we were all flies caught in a spider's web, waiting to be wrapped up and slowly crushed to our death.

Reflections

- What were some of the best and worst experiences from high school or your teenage years? They may be actual memories of specific situations or just a recollection of feelings or general experiences during this time.
- What feelings do these experiences bring up for you when you think about them? How raw are they in your emotional memory?
- How did these experiences contribute to the way you felt about yourself (your self-confidence) when you finished high school?

Somewhere within that struggle, all of the growth that occurs during those pinnacle years strikes me as both fierce and tender, beautifully alive and triumphant. It is a rite of passage to experience these years in all of their grisliness and glory. We emerge from this deeply traumatic and yet mutually collective experience that both separates and binds us to our counterparts, and then we are adults, ready to enter the world and become actual human beings. Suddenly, how we see ourselves within our comfortable microcosm is less important, and how quickly we are willing to stop wallowing and grow outside of our comfort zone becomes essential.

Look, it is possible that you were far more adjusted as a person than I was and you cruised straight out of high school into adulthood with grace and ease. I can just imagine you with your long, tanned legs and sleek hair, your steady boyfriend and your clear ambition. The rest of us, however, tumbled out of the high school gates like the Lost Boys with one eyebrow, very little poise and a healthy disrespect for authority and the future. Having the vague sense of being thrust out into something bigger than we could really grasp, we blindly stumbled, or were forced, on to the next thing.

You may, or may not, have met this situation with the same resistance, denial and fear that I did.

I grieved and mourned the loss of high school, quite atypically given that it was such a minefield of inner and outer conflict. But it was a minefield that I had delicately learned to navigate. I had grown comfortable with, almost fond of, the careful treading and I didn't yet feel ready to be pushed out of my patch of land. School finished, then there were Schoolies and the Christmas holidays where I spent the majority of the time drunk or moping in equal amounts of boredom and denial, buying me just enough time to consider my plan of attack for the next stage of life. Maybe for you it was a university degree. A clever few took a gap year to work and travel and *grow*.

I'd achieved a less-than-stellar academic performance due to my active social calendar so I fluffed around for a while, finally settling on a TAFE course in Tourism and Event Management. It sounded like a 'How To' on travel and fancy events – the perfect combo. Unfortunately, there was actual work involved in completing the qualification so a few months later I dropped out. I desperately craved freedom in my new adult life so I found a full-time reception position at a residential real estate firm (with the help of my mum's colleague – it's all about who you know). I wasn't sure where it would lead but I trundled along with the idea that at least a job would fund my lifestyle.

I got my driver's licence, after a couple of mandatory failed attempts. Around the same time, I had moved out of home and in with a friend into a cheap little apartment on the train line. It was pretty dingy and disgusting but only after we moved in. Oh, the glorious feeling of ducking down to the twenty-four-hour Night Owl to buy cigarettes and Pineapple Lumps without my concerned mother saying, "Where are you going? Who with?" Not to mention watching whatever the hell I wanted on TV. True independence.

Over the next few months, I rode on the high of doing what I wanted, whenever I wanted. Of course, I still popped home to see Mum, a five-minute drive away and always with a full fridge of leftovers. At work, I had started moving past the initial awkwardness of adult conversations with my new colleagues and the nauseating fear of transferring a call to the wrong person. Thanks to some tough-love training, I was even becoming a valued member of the team. I was learning about the daunting concept of business and how the world actually runs. My neural pathways were positively *zinging* with all of the new information. I had a purpose and I was moving forward.

There were a few gnawing feelings that kept bugging me. One was commonly, 'I'm hungry, better go to Mum's house.' More poignantly, perhaps, was the realisation, 'I'm lonely all of the time.' Whenever I was alone, I would fall into this intense, depressive-like state, which was a mixture of fear, self-hatred and loathing of everyone and everything. I continued to follow the usual routine – wake up, go to work, come home, watch TV and go to bed. Often, I would go out at night with friends to bars and clubs, drink, dance and go home – maybe by myself, and maybe not. Rinse and repeat.

I felt empty. My friends seemed happy and joyous and free. I thought that maybe it was because many of them had boyfriends and I didn't. Or that they were just inherently cooler than me and more accustomed to life on the outside (of high school). Maybe they were struggling just as much as I was and I didn't realise it. I lacked the ability to identify and articulate what was going on inside me, so I didn't feel like I had anyone I could talk to at that time.

Most of my friends were studying at university so they seemed to all be making new friends. Because I so strongly doubted my own self-worth, I was easily threatened by new people. Changes were clearly taking place, whether I liked it or not, stirring colossal insecurity within me. I didn't necessarily want things to stay the same but it was too much, too fast and I couldn't (or wouldn't) keep up.

I was anxious and scared of all of these new experiences. There seemed to be a lot of things that others felt ready to do and I didn't. Mainly meeting new people and making new friends. I was meeting friends of friends left, right and centre. But what did I have to offer a new group? I found it hard to sell myself to strangers. I didn't even know who I was and I didn't have much to say. I was like a strange mirage – there but not there. I took a back seat in conversations and I didn't expect anyone to ask or care about who I was. In fact, I preferred it if they didn't. I just bought myself another drink, kept on dancing and allowed the focus to remain on my more extroverted and interesting friends.

There was still so much bitchiness between friends at that time. Sometimes I would hear about friends doing things without me and that would hurt. I have no doubt that I participated in the backstabbing with absolute gusto, like everyone else, but being left out of plans definitely cemented my lack of self-esteem. This was prior to the bombardment of social media so at least one saving grace was that I wasn't faced with the photographic evidence of everyone having a good time without me.

Instead of being honest about the drama within my friendships, I kept separating myself from my friends, telling myself that I was a bigger person, that I only needed myself and that they weren't worth my time if they were going to play emotional games. This was a solid lesson I was taught by my mum as I was growing up. "Just ignore them," she would say. A strong moral example in independence and dignity – certainly important for a young woman to learn. But, unfortunately, I didn't have anyone else, so cutting myself off from all of my friends only set me up for more loneliness. I felt completely isolated and continued to build up emotional barriers.

This is not to say that I sat at home and did nothing. I wouldn't let anyone beat me. So I sought out other lone soldiers and misfits in my social sphere, usually guys because I just found them easier to hang out with and they were always keen to drink. One group of guy friends that I hung out with on some weekends actually called me 'Rent a

Crowd' (*affectionately*, I'm sure) because I always met up with them on my own. Even though we had plenty of laughs, I still lacked deep connections. And I was avoiding my own company at all costs.

At the time, I wasn't strong enough to really recognise that this was the beginning of my wake-up call. But instead of taking note of how I was feeling, I continued to power through because that was what I was taught to do – soldier on. To be honest, I had no idea what I was soldiering on towards.

Somewhere within the next ten years I planned to be Miranda Kerr – hot, have at least a hundred grand in the bank, own a house, be with the love of my life, and just be generally Okay.

All I knew in that moment was that I didn't have any of those things, and I certainly wasn't Okay, even if I had ticked off most of society's boxes on what it means to be a fully-functioning adult. Roof over my head – tick. Working – tick. Enough money to buy a cheeseburger and cask of wine – tick.

I can't tell you how disappointed I felt knowing that this was what Life amounted to. I finally got out of high school alive but everything still sucked. Sure, sure, I was taught at school that the Real World was a tough, cold-hearted place but I never really believed that coming from teachers. It was hard to respect and listen to life advice from such a strange bunch of adults who held their students in such heinous contempt. I guess, thanks to them, I knew some examples of what I *didn't* want – to end up as clearly miserable as they were.

But what did I want? Was I the only one that felt these intense feelings of longing and emptiness?

Reflections

- How well were you prepared for leaving high school and entering adulthood? Think back to some of your emotional experiences during this time.
- Did you find the transition easy or difficult? What would have made it easier? What/who was supportive during that time of your life?
- Was your next step after high school (i.e. work, study or travel) an easy decision? What would you do differently if you had your time over again? Why?
- If you haven't left high school yet, consider how you feel about your current experiences. What are some of the highs and lows? Who is supportive and who makes things more difficult? What is your next step in life going to look like? How do you want to feel when you take the next step?

Moving forward...

Instead of wallowing in my emptiness and confusion, I needed to stop and listen to my heart. Powering on in denial was not helping. I was experiencing an identity crisis of sorts. I didn't know who I was or what I wanted. As I was moving from my teenage to adult years, it was becoming more obvious that I could only rely on myself for answers and this scared the shit out of me. It was time to accept some of the crucial lessons being shoved in my face like I was a clown and truth was a pie.

Unfortunately for me, it took a few more years of dogged denial and internal bewilderment for me to figure out how to accept that things weren't right. I was stubborn and emotionally immature. In retrospect, I realise how much easier it would have been to stop fighting than to keep forcing myself to be someone I wasn't. I most certainly would have been able to smile more and worry less. But things panned out for me the way they needed to, in order for me to learn what was necessary – just as they will for you.

There's no need to force it but it might be helpful to consider how you are feeling about your own identity, now that you are no longer a child. Acceptance of yourself and your personal situation will allow you to make supportive decisions for your life as you move forward. We will begin to discuss how you can move past whatever you have been through, whatever it is you are going through now and any emotional blocks or negative beliefs that challenge your ability to live life fully.

Your background may be similar to mine or it may be completely different. It doesn't matter. The feelings that you are experiencing and the core of your desires are universal. By considering your own story, you can begin to heal wounds and accept past hurts so that they no longer hold power over your adult life. You will start to build new unconscious thoughts, feelings and self-beliefs that are aligned with where you are headed, not where you've been.

They say you can't change the past, and this may be true. However, you can reframe your own perspective. With a fresh outlook, your life becomes your own again.

Reflections

Contemplate the following questions as we move through the following chapters:

- How well are you in touch with who you are? Do you like what you see?
- What do you want out of life?
- Are you experiencing feelings of loneliness or lack of confidence?
- What are the thoughts contributing to your state of mind?
- What are the impacts of your behaviour at this time?

You don't need the answers to these questions now but consider the thoughts and feelings that come up for you as you read them. The answers may become more obvious to you as we discuss the underlying aspects of being stuck in an emotional and situational rut, and how to move forward in your life.

Chapter Two
All Roads Lead to Rome

I'm a big girl now...

The transition from teenager to adult tends to throw all of our baggage into the spotlight. It can be a challenging and lonely time of life where our unconscious negative beliefs from childhood are forced onto centre stage. It's hard not to feel sorry for yourself, the rough trot you've been dealt and all. No one really understands what you're going through and what has tormented your past. Even if you wanted to talk about your problems, you couldn't. You wouldn't know where to find the words. There are too many memories, too many kicks in the cooch that have got you to this point.

Pain doesn't always stem from something that has been done to you, but from an event or an established behavioural pattern that you have accepted as normal from childhood. Even if the event happened a long time ago, it can become ingrained into your psyche and affect the way you relate to the world. As we grow up, we are all forced to get by with whatever skills we have, based on what we learn from our parents, our friends and our own personality traits.

Let's Talk About It...

There can be some pretty heavy self-learning that comes from looking back into the past. If you know that this could be triggering for you, undertake this with the support of a counsellor or health professional. If you have never spoken to someone like this before, here's what to do:

- Google counsellors or psychologists in your local area;
- Choose a couple that give you a good vibe and contact them to enquire about the cost and timeframe of an appointment, and whether they offer a government or private health rebate;
- Some counsellors will not be eligible for a rebate but may be priced accordingly so that you will not be too much out of pocket. If you choose to see a practitioner that provides the rebate, you may first need to see a GP and receive a referral or some formal documentation in order to claim this. You may also have success with a practitioner qualified in areas other than counselling, such as naturopathy or hypnotherapy);
- Book an appointment with a counsellor, psychologist or other health professional that makes you feel comfortable and is priced suitably for your needs.

When I was a child, my parents had a less-than-happy marriage and subsequently divorced. It felt a little surreal because the family structure to which I'd become accustomed was changing and even though I knew that my parents didn't seem to enjoy each other's company, this felt challenging for someone as sheltered as nine-year-old me. My dad broke the news to me that he was leaving with tears rolling down his face, sitting on the back stairs of my childhood home. I remember holding his hand and telling him that it was going to be okay. My mum was as strong as she could be during this time, even though she felt like she had failed me and my sisters by allowing our home to become a broken one.

I felt like I had to continue to be strong for my parents while they were dealing with this issue. I knew it was hard for everyone and didn't want to make it harder. Conflict was never openly discussed in our house so there were many moments of silent tension and sadness when I felt I had to mediate, being a classic middle child. I wanted to be strong for my mum and so it seemed natural to paste on a brave face and put my own feelings in a secret box. The confused child in me tried to make sense of the years of ugliness that ensued but, ultimately, I forced it all into a compartment and disconnected my outer self as far away from it as I could.

Over time, I developed the sense that no-one really understood me because there was a huge chunk of pain inside that I had hidden for so long. I never consciously realised that this pattern continued all throughout my life. It grew to be a deeply ingrained belief of mine that no-one knew the 'real me'. This made it harder for my family, friends or partners to get to know what was going on inside me and limited my ability to communicate my thoughts and feelings.

Knowing that I couldn't outwardly display the real me fed directly into my lack of confidence and the belief that I must not be worth getting to know. These emotional barriers extended to my inner self as well – I stopped trusting my internal voice and lost the ability to identify what I was feeling within myself at the time. I spent so much time confused and in pain; a vicious cycle which blocked my personal growth and happiness.

It wasn't necessarily the situation itself but my own beliefs and individual reaction to it that took me down this path. Childhood has a wealth of instances where pain, no matter how small or seemingly insignificant to someone else, can manifest into negative beliefs about who we are and how the world is. We are all individuals that deal with things in different ways. And, there are three sides to every story – my version, your version and the truth.

Reflections

- How did your parents or guardians communicate with you when you were a child? Were you privy to information (maybe too much) or were bad things swept under the rug?
- How did this affect your ability to understand and deal with negative events as you grew up?
- Consider a few negative experiences or sources of pain from your childhood, the first ones that come into your head. Think about the ways in which they affected you at the time, and what feelings come up for you when you think about them now. Are you able to laugh at the memories or do they still hurt?
- If you are struggling to think of memories, it may be helpful to talk to a sibling about their experiences. Be aware that this can bring up some uncomfortable conversations.

Family conflict often relates back to complicated adult relationships and the depth of character of our mother and father – things that we cannot fully appreciate with our simple, young minds.

When we are young or in pain, or both, it's near impossible for us to really understand perspectives other than our own because of our limited understanding of what's really happening. This does not make our pain any less real.

It's what we do with the pain that matters. Once acknowledging that it exists, do we face it or simply allow it to fuel our blame and poor choices?

As you are discovering who you are and where you fit in this world, it makes sense that there are going to be challenging moments where you feel unsafe or unworthy to keep advancing successfully. You might find yourself heading down one path and then realise that it's not where you want to be. You're still figuring out what feels satisfying and fulfilling. At the moment, you are probably content with the thought of having more money and things, cooler friends, and wilder experiences. The big picture might not seem as important as all of the small pictures that you collect for your Insty and Snapchat accounts.

Even if you aren't looking ahead to the future, making your everyday life more enjoyable and emotionally stable depends on dealing with the past. Emotional upheaval, trauma, negative beliefs about the self, unhealthy relationship patterns (or all of the above) need to be looked upon as stepping stones to the person that we are today. By consciously identifying and accepting the areas in our life that hurt, they no longer control the way we feel, think and behave.

It's hard to sit with painful feelings for too long, to have the courage to face what was, so that you might start to welcome what could be. When you are able to slowly undress your negative beliefs, until they are stripped bare and you realise where they have come from, it becomes clear that they actually have very little power over your future. By making the unconscious conscious, you are allowing acceptance into your life and that's when you start the process of healing from the past.

Without looking inside ourselves to take note of what's going on, we go around and around in circles wondering why we don't feel happy even though we just bought that new thing that we thought we wanted. Life becomes a series of events orchestrated purely to distract ourselves from the pain we hide inside. No matter how far or how fast you run, the past always finds a way of catching up with you. Destructive patterns get carried through from childhood memories into adult relationships, whether you like it or not, and this can show up in your home life, your social life or your work life, and in the boundaries you create in your relationships.

Reflections

- What are some of the ways you distract yourself from thinking about painful things? Examples might include food, booze, exercise, watching television, social media, gaming or even fuelling drama within friendships and relationships.
- How do these things stop you from thinking or feeling deeply?
- What do you think the long-term effects are of avoiding painful experiences and negative beliefs?

Acceptance and forgiveness...

Dealing with what has happened to you and understanding the bigger picture takes you out of thinking like a victim of your circumstances, and into a position of strength where you have the power to decide how you want it to affect your life. An empowered perspective means raising yourself above the pain, just for a moment, in order to take a higher view and see more sides of the story than just your own. Acknowledgement of events makes pain easier to accept; acceptance leads to understanding, forgiveness and ultimately letting go of the aching feelings of pain and betrayal you are holding on to.

You may spend a good portion of your time thinking about how painful things are, and it might even define how you see yourself. You may not feel ready to let go of the many ways you've been hurt just yet. The concept of forgiveness can be particularly unpalatable when you are still angry. Feeling the continuous sting of past events especially from family and friends that we love and trust the most, makes us less likely to want to let them off the hook with forgiveness. We can't bear to give them the satisfaction of getting off so lightly and we want justice to be served. We end up suffering for far longer over the memory of whatever happened.

It was Buddha who said that holding on to resentment is like drinking poison and expecting the other person to die. This might be true but we can't all be as accepting and forgiving as Zen messengers of God, can we? We can't just absolve that person from the terrible things they have done, or the way that they've made us feel. They should feel the wrath of our grudge for life as penance for what they have put us through.

It's true that the process of acceptance and forgiveness can be just as painful, if not more so, as the original wound. Peeling back the layers to get to the core of pain can mean facing some uncomfortable memories. However, if we skip this part and just hope that by refusing to address it, it will simply go away, then the ghosts of the past will undoubtedly come back to haunt us when we are unsuspecting.

Steps to Forgiveness

- Identify your pain–articulate the exact situation and your thoughts and feelings about the situation and person/people involved.
- Get perspective–understand that the pain you are carrying is from your own hurt feelings, rather than the actual situation from minutes, hours or years ago. The other person/people involved have their own version of the story which you may not agree with, but it can help understand where they were coming from in order to emotionally separate yourself from the outcome of the situation.
- Make the decision to forgive–forgiveness is for you and only you, in order to make peace with the reality of a situation. Commit to your decision. You will inevitably feel anger or hurt continue to rise up from time to time, but make the conscious choice to tell your mind, your body and your heart that it is time to move on.
- Live an amazing life–not out of spite but from your genuine passionate spirit. That is the best revenge, after all.

A word on forgiveness...

Do not mistake forgiveness with submission. In no way does forgiveness mean that you must accept this person back into your life, or that you must willingly hand over your trusting heart to them ever again. Forgiveness is loving yourself enough to say, "That happened and it hurt but I am willing to move on."

Sometimes, it isn't always possible to continue relationships with people that have had a toxic effect on our lives. Children of emotional, verbal and physical abuse might feel pressured to forgive and forget, let go and move on. As people, we have an innate desire to set our relationship right with our parents because, from an evolutionary perspective, they have the ability to provide protection, food, love and other basic needs for survival. Biologically, we are connected and they are tough ties to cut. This attachment sees us seeking their love and approval through our behaviour, even if they are not good parents.

Depending on the original issue, forgiveness may be achieved if both parent and child are willing. When we start to grow up and gain a better understanding of relationship dynamics, thinking back to painful experiences with our parents displays the wrongness of their behaviour or the situation in neon flashing lights. It's not okay that your dad continually told you that you were useless and wouldn't amount to anything. It's not helpful that your mum suffered severe depression and wouldn't get out of bed for days at a time. You shouldn't have had to walk on eggshells every time your parents were in the same room together.

You've grown up and now you're looking back at those days with resentment and self-pity. You've identified what hurt you. The question is, is Mum still emotionally manipulating you into believing that you're a bad daughter? Does Dad still drink and become angry and abusive over the smallest detail? If you still feel like these issues are ongoing and they will continually hold this power over you, then realise that you don't always win by trying to be the bigger person and continuing to uphold the relationship, just because they are your parents. If you want to move past those horrid and confusing years, you can't let yourself become stuck forever in that dynamic.

Of course, it can be incredibly difficult and painful to cut ties with family. There is often guilt involved if you are the one walking away. The feeling of giving up or refusing to fix what went wrong plays on your mind. But, there is also relief because you can only fix what is yours. You still have to be met halfway. Acknowledgement of guilt or acceptance of wrongdoing from the other person may be the first step to forgiveness and reconciliation. But first you must be strong enough in yourself to know that you can walk away, that you are the one who is setting the physical, mental and emotional boundaries and will no longer enable that person to hurt you in that way.

If you feel like you are carrying pain and hurtful experiences into the present, particularly from any kind of abuse, I would thoroughly recommend talking to a counsellor about these experiences. Identifying trauma is the first step to understanding what underlying factors are holding you back from becoming a happy and successful person. Once you understand the emotional patterns and negative beliefs, you can deal with them through acceptance, growth and healing. You may also consider cutting ties with a toxic or manipulative relationship, or work together with that person to understand where they were coming from at the time, and then move forward.

If it isn't that cut and dried and you can't just walk away, or you would like to cut ties but you are unable to for a particular reason, talk to a counsellor, psychologist or health professional about how you might enforce a boundary on your parent (or guardian, or any person of influence) so that their negative behaviour doesn't affect you in the same way that it did when you were a child. Bringing old relationship dynamics into adulthood can lead to anxiety, depression, substance abuse, anger management issues, unhealthy eating patterns leading to disorders or obesity, negative beliefs about the self, unhealthy relationship patterns and other chronic diseases.

Respect yourself enough to know when it is time to separate yourself, even if you still have to have contact with that person and only mental and emotional separation is possible.

Sweeping it under the rug...

If you came from a family that drummed into you that you shouldn't talk about how you feel or about anything negative that is happening, it can be very confrontational to open the floodgates of your feelings about events of the past. This is why it might be helpful to go through the process in a measured and supportive way with someone who'll objectively listen without being personally or emotionally involved. Someone who will allow you to figure it all out for yourself, and won't subject you to their opinion while you are feeling vulnerable. This is your opportunity to identify your memories, your thoughts and feelings about them, and to challenge and shift negative self-talk that you are bringing into the present day. You may even feel strong enough to start a journal and begin this process on your own.

Even if you had a lovely upbringing (which, on the whole, I believe I did), childhood is an impressionable time and we are all human. No parent is perfect. No matter how seemingly insignificant the memory or situation, any pain you hold inside is worth exploring. This process will move you from victim to empowered survivor, proving to yourself that you are strong enough to define yourself separately to your inner pain. You are not what has happened to you.

Instead, you will begin to appreciate where you have come from and accept your background rather than be embarrassed by it. You may forgive, or at the very least accept, parental shortcomings, dysfunction or absence. You may even gain enough wisdom to be able to understand what your parents were experiencing at the time and the reasons they fell short in their responsibilities.

Possibly the most painful yet enlightening part of growing up is dealing with all of the things that have shaped who we are, throughout our life, both negative and positive. The world needs your courage and your strength. Your personal experiences, and the skills that result from them, are a gift that you bring into the world, not a limitation.

Own your past.

Reflections

- What kind of relationship did your parents have with each other? If your parents are no longer in a relationship together, consider the relationship between your mother/father and their partner. If your parent was not in a relationship, how did this affect them/your household?
- How has the influence of your parents' relationship or lack of relationship affected your idea of relationships? Have they had an effect on your beliefs about romantic relationships? For example, 'Men cheat', 'Love is hard work', 'Marriage is an outdated convention', etc.
- What character traits do you aspire to replicate from the people that influenced your childhood, i.e. parent, guardian, grandparent? What character traits were you exposed to during childhood that you see as flawed, or hope not to carry into your own adulthood?
- Are there specific events or instances from childhood or your teenage years that are still causing you pain? If so, it may be helpful to start a journal or speak to a counsellor in order to articulate as an adult:
    1. Exactly what happened;
    2. How you felt when the event occurred;
    3. How you feel about it now.
- Why it is still difficult to let go? List ten negative beliefs about yourself–your abilities.

- If you are planning to raise a family one day, what differences do you hope to achieve in your style of parenting, or the lifestyle that
you wish to provide for your children?
- personality or physical appearance How did your upbringing contribute to your thoughts about yourself? Do they exist in spite of your parents' love and support, or do they correlate in some way with how you were raised?

Chapter Three
All My Friends are Vampires

As teenagers, our world revolves around what other people think of us. At any age, I was always sensitive and impressionable to the opinions of other people, particularly anyone whom I believed to be cooler and more popular. My friends in high school were a group of attractive, outspoken and outgoing girls who seemed to have shit all figured out. I faked a strong sense of self to match theirs, intending to look knowledgeable and mature but no doubt appearing naïve and petty instead.

I tried my best to build genuine friendships but, to be honest, I wasn't very good at it. The true basis of a friendship is mutual love, respect, honesty, trust and support. When I was younger, I had suffered some bullying which fuelled my determination to fit in and be liked. I had a deep desire to be important and special, and I thought to achieve that I had to be cool and beautiful. Unluckily for me, Nerd Chic wasn't in fashion at the time so the glasses I had worn since nine years old felt like an obvious 'Loser' sign on my face. As did my braces, girlish body and mousy hair.

My desire to prove my worth to others meant that I spent too much time trying to impress people and not enough time loving them.

So there I was, thrust into this pecking order with everyone else, fighting to be recognised. The caste system seemed to be set by the prettiest or most conniving girls in the grade, and you were only acceptable if you fitted into a neat little category – Funny, Pretty, Rich or Smart. Even better if you ticked more than one of these boxes. I initially tried to be myself as much as possible and when that didn't work, I adapted to be what I felt I needed to be to make friends and be accepted. I didn't feel like I ticked any of the required boxes and tried to be all of these things by association instead. What I didn't realise was that you can't be friends with someone purely because you want something that they have (looks, money or status) and you hang around them in the hope that it will rub off on you. Friendship does not work that way.

<u>Reflections</u>

- How did you learn to make friends? Did you naturally gravitate towards the people around you due to common interests, geographical location or were there other factors?
- In what ways did you adapt your own personality, to become more 'cool' or 'likeable'?
- Do you find it easy to be the 'real you' around your friends? How impressionable are you to the thoughts, feelings and opinions of others?

Incommunicado...

After school finished, my core friendship group stayed pretty much the same, consisting of girls from my school as well as a few stragglers from other schools. We kept largely the same relationship dynamics. In our haste to become *mature* and *experienced,* there was still plenty of competitive clambering against each other. We began to split up into mini-groups where there were two or three of us who were 'best friends'. A few started romantic relationships which automatically meant less opportunities to spend time with them.

Suddenly, we no longer spent all day together and maintaining the friendship required actual effort to keep up communication and social activity. Apart from showing up to school, participating in whatever drama or joke was going down and writing the odd letter during class, I had never actually had to *try* before. This was new territory and I suddenly felt like the popular façade I had portrayed was a sham. My insecurities flared as I felt out of the loop and ostracised.

Embarrassingly enough, I was so stubborn and indignant that I found myself playing one-sided mind games where I would test each friend to see how long it would be before they called me to see how I was doing. When they did call, I would spin a web of bullshit about how busy I had been, but yes I could probably, just now, fit them in to my schedule. I sought out random friends outside of my inner circle to supplement my social existence and ensure that I was remaining relevant, active and interesting.

A cycle existed where my friends were constantly confirming the way I felt about myself. If I didn't hear from anyone, I would feel like such a loser. I moped around, resenting my own company and filled my time with listening to music and walking to the park to smoke cigarettes. When we did hang out, I always felt an emptiness. I filled my void momentarily by dedicating as much of my energy as possible to whatever drama was happening in my friends' worlds. I tried to be supportive but also resented them on the sly. I listened but I judged. I put my own concerns at the bottom of the priority list but secretly wallowed there. I assumed no one cared what I was experiencing internally.

Confrontation...

I was never strong enough to have a proper fight with my friends or at least say what was on my mind, partly because I had no idea how to handle confrontation, and partly because I thought that if we had a fight, we had to stop being friends and then I would literally have no friends. I thought that the price I had to pay for having 'cool' friends was that they wouldn't always be there for me when I needed them. They were self-absorbed in their lives and I was self-absorbed in my pain and determination to be the victim.

It is important to acknowledge that my friends were not bad people. Despite the flakiness, we had a lot of fun. We experienced the occasional flash of meaningful connection, fuelling my desire to keep it up. They could be supportive provided I actually spoke up about what was happening in my life. It may have been a bit of a cesspit of drama and bitchiness, but I participated alongside them in all of the good, the bad and the ugly. Our friendships were part love, part laughter and part jealousy, perpetuated by common insecurities and amplified by alcohol.

That being said, there were times when I was torn between persevering and walking away. I did actually care about my friends but I knew there should be more to friendship than this. At the time, I put up with it because I felt it was 'better the devil you know than the devil you don't'. My mum would say, "Ignore them. Make new friends," etc. etc. Well, to me, it never seemed that simple. Making new friends is difficult when everyone is still largely grouped in the same way as high school. Walking away from that kind of history you share feels like cutting off your arm. Not to mention actually admitting defeat against friendships I had been fighting to keep for five or more years.

If you're anything like me, you're sensitive to the opinions of others, so even when something isn't right you avoid any type of conflict. I generally find it easier to bite my tongue and put up with a fairly large helping of irritation and injustice, retreating into myself rather than encouraging others to understand, and therefore judge me on, my feelings and opinions. Part of me wanted to be dignified and accept that maybe I just needed to find nicer, more invested friends.

But it's not as if they were terrible people. I knew this, despite the fact that I felt lonely and rejected most of the time.

Reflections

Consider your own friendships:

- Are they one-sided or do you feel that they are a two-way street?
- How worthy do you feel of supportive and loving friendships?
- Are you clinging to a certain dynamic in your friendships because you are afraid to demand more?

It can be so hard to know where to draw the line in friendships, especially when you are still running the negative internal dialogue from high school that the opinions of others matter and you'll be a complete failure if you can't make everyone see how great you are. It feels that talking about these issues with your friends is unlikely to resolve the situation with a hug and stronger bond between you. You can't risk losing the friends you do have because you will then have no social life at all.

I felt like I had only two options – grin and bear it while I continued to feel like I was being walked over and mistreated, or walk away from my friends completely while I blamed them for their wrongdoing. I was almost prepared to cut and run, wasting the years of friendship and diminishing it all into nothing. The third option, I realised after some long, lonely years, was choosing to look inward, own up to my vulnerability and start doing things differently at my end.

I realise now, with the benefit of hindsight, that I had placed the whole situation outside of my personal control. My life and happiness were basically hanging on the decisions of others and whether they chose to call me, to invite me, to care about me, to know the real me. I was allowing this dynamic to continue because I was too stubborn to accept that something needed to change. It was unconsciously easier to remain the victim in my friendships and blame my friends for all of my pain and confusion.

Taking back control means taking responsibility...

No one is going to swoop in and change your relationships for you. It might be a little bit of work but it is possible to improve your friendships by understanding and owning the role you are playing in your friendships. It literally changes everything.

How do you positively contribute to your friendships? What hand do you play in perpetuating the negative stuff? Accepting what kind of friend you are now highlights how you can be a better friend. Learning how you can be a better friend also articulates what you desire in your own friendships, which reinforces what you are willing to accept and not willing to accept within your relationships. This process improves your sense of self, positively influences your confidence and has a flow-on effect in all areas of life.

Friendships are actually able to evolve. Ten years later, my group of close friends remains largely the same as during those shitty years, albeit the dynamics have changed and I no longer put energy into malicious, manipulative or exhausting people. I have loads of new friends that I have picked up over the years – people who may not share that same sense of history but share common values, interests and outlooks on life.

Setting up strong, positive dynamics in our relationships is essential to get out of a friendship what we put in. We need supportive relationships in our lives that keep us connected, help us to grow and become more compassionate human beings.

Find Your Tribe

Our friendships usually form with those whom we share the most history; however, as you move through life don't be afraid to collect new friends and build meaningful relationships with others. New friendships that are supportive and uplifting can be found with people who have similar outlooks on life, values, interests and connections.

Making new friends can be awkward but if you meet a kindred spirit, don't be shy–ask them on a 'date' or tell them you will add them on Facebook. It's much more awkward to get home and realise that you've missed out on a possible new connection.

Lean on me…

Things inevitably happen in our lives that we need help to get through, and someone to talk to who will let us ugly-cry on their shoulder without the fear of being judged for our problems or feelings. A true friend is someone who supports us, even when we fuck up at life. They are there for the hardship and they are most certainly there for the good times.

When you are trying to grow and develop as a person, the last thing you need is a friend who constantly reminds you of who you were in high school rather than encouraging you to bloom into a beautiful adult flower. Friends shouldn't be trying to keep us stuck in our insecurities because it serves their own selfish needs. When we are younger, we will often put up with more shit than we are willing to as we grow up. If there is an imbalance within a friendship, you may be expending more than your fair share of time and energy to keep it alive. The dynamics that you set up in the friendship when you were younger may continue for longer than they should, leaving you lonely and resentful, and feeling like you're back in Grade Ten, contending for the cool kids' attention.

We've all had at least one friend who drains our emotional resources so significantly that we need a power nap after seeing them. They are usually the most fun, most crazy and most connected friend we have. These same friends are often also the most opinionated, influential and draining of our time and energy with their drama and neediness. These friends are often hard work to keep in touch with and you are almost always the one to contact them, rarely hearing from them otherwise. And when you do catch up, you listen, advise and empathise until your ears bleed. You go home to digest their complex stories while shaking your head, feeling a combination of frustration, emptiness and boredom with your own life. Next week you call them and do it all over again.

Our relationships mostly reflect the relationship that we have with ourselves. If you are constantly seeking approval from friends by going the extra mile even though you don't receive the same in return, it may be because internally you have not given yourself approval and deserved attention. When you don't respect yourself enough to enforce proper boundaries in your relationships, it becomes easier to focus your attention on high maintenance people that suck the life from your loins. Friends like this will take advantage of your sensitive nature and will use it to improve the way they feel about themselves. You are each providing a diversion to each other from being real with yourselves.

You don't need to live vicariously through their drama-filled existence. You are interesting, you are important and you are special. Yes, you.

If you are able to identify the qualities that you expect and desire within your friendships then you are more likely to invite healthy relationships into your life, either by meeting new people or evolving a current relationship to be stronger and more supportive for both of you. You will learn how to be a better friend, and give these qualities more willingly and openly. In existing friendships, consider how you might gently mend your relationships. Setting healthy boundaries is essential to ensuring you are taking care of yourself first before taking on the problems and drama of draining people.

There is a delicate balance of give and take in any friendship and you know instinctively when this line has been crossed too many times. Sometimes toxic relationships do need to end. Other times, acceptance of how your friend behaves in a relationship with you and their capability of showing love is enough to set the emotional boundary so that they can no longer take advantage of your kind heart. Part of being a good friend is also your own ability to build up your friend's strengths rather than focusing on their weaknesses. Setting the emotional boundary and allowing each other to grow and learn within the friendship provides an opportunity to grow closer and create a long-lasting friendship.

Evolving Relationship Dynamics

- Define what you want in that friend–not every person in your life has to be a 'best friend' or someone that gets you completely. Accept that some friends will only be there for the good times and that's okay, as long as you are not placing your needs in their incapable hands. Of course, you should be able to expect that some friends will provide you with a deep connection, support and love (and vice versa), and that these are necessary components in order to maintain fulfilling friendships.
- Be realistic with your expectations–are you asking for more than this person is willing to give? Consider the type of person that they are before investing your time and energy. Are they capable of being who you need right now? Have they had very close friendships before? If so, what qualities make their other close friendships shine? Are they an extrovert with many shallow friendships? Have they learned to trust easily throughout their life or not at all? Does this person portray the same version of themselves around everyone, or do they change personality with their mood or accompanying crowd?
- Cultivate the good stuff–focus on what syncs you to this friend and puts this friendship into a positive flow. What qualities attract you to this friend? Let go of old 'stuff' as much as you can. There is no use holding onto resentment from

- previous years of hardship within your relationships. In order to move forward, and sustain friendships that you are in control of, you must take control of your emotions and therefore your future. If there are things that you cannot forgive in someone, focus your energy on building your relationship with someone different.
- Be realistic about the person that you are–in order for a relationship to be successful, you must be yourself. Your friend will see straight through you if you are trying to be something that you are not. You will end up lonely and resentful every time. Make sure you can identify the difference between encouraging the positive aspects of a friendship to build a stronger bond, and railroading your own needs for the purpose of pleasing another person. Be honest about what needs you want to fulfil with this friendship. Because, otherwise, what you end up with will be an empty shell of what you really want.
- Genuinely put in your share of the work and give it time–you can't control anything but your share of the friendship. If your friend is not responding to your efforts of building a deeper connection, then it is your responsibility to question why. And it is not because you are an ugly, boring loser–please do not let that be your default state of mind if things don't go your way. You have much to offer as a friend! But perhaps it isn't a good fit, just as we are attracted romantically to some and not others.

Maybe your friend is trying to tell you with their subtle rejection, "It's not you, it's me..." Maybe your strengths don't match up with their needs. Maybe they don't even know what they need. Then again, maybe it'll be great.

Maintenance–some friendships will hum along effortlessly and others will require more work. More than anything, expect joy from your friendships. It is not necessarily an entitlement but a sacred contract in which two inner worlds begin to be shared. Put in the work and you will both reap the rewards.

The role of trust...

Sometimes our inherent lack of confidence and self-worth feeds into paranoia and the expectation that your friends will inevitably fail you at some point, just because everything feels uncertain and it seems reasonable enough that something terrible is probably coming. You resent your friends because of what they might do, purely because you care for them and have placed your trust in their hands.

For Example:

Maybe a friend has neglected to invite you somewhere, or has bitched about you behind your back, or has consistently dodged your calls, texts and making plans with you to catch up…

- Don't jump to the conclusion that you're a loser and everybody hates you;
- Try to understand your friend's motivations–ask them calmly, if possible;
- Consider whether this is an isolated instance or whether it has happened before. If it has happened before, when? How often?
- Was this simply an oversight, a personality clash, or is this friend deliberately trying to tear you down?
- What are the reactions of your other friends?

But when a situation arises where someone gets hurt, we don't need to fall apart. It feels impossible but you can actually take the situation for what it is and move on.

Friendships are made to be shared. The thing about friendship is that you can only control your fifty per cent share. The other fifty per cent should be picked up by the friend on the other side. Sometimes we are human and drop the ball. Maybe you will decide that a second chance for your friend is warranted and you're willing to allow your trust in this person to cautiously build up again over time. At the end of the day, nobody is perfect and while you are treading the muddy mangroves of growing up and into an established human being, you must accept that you will encounter the character flaws of your friends. You also have your own to get to know and love.

Having said that, sometimes relationships are irreparable and cutting ties is the only way forward. Maybe you don't want to deal with the bullshit and it's easier not to have this person in your life. If your so-called friend fucked your boyfriend or did some other such terrible thing, then don't believe for one minute that they have any regard for your feelings. If you are afraid to voice your true feelings without prejudice from your friends, then they don't respect who you are.

Life is too short to be tainted by relationships that crush your spirit.

As you shape who you are, friendships will eventually evolve into something a little less dependent and more supportive, provided you allow them to. You must be flexible enough to let go of your perception of past wrongdoing and start afresh. It's okay, in fact it's necessary, to change who you were in high school into somebody that you're proud of, somebody who has a voice and uses it. You're an adult and you're free. Shake off that oppressive weight of adolescence from your shoulders.

Friendships should not be a battlefield. Defend yourself if you must but don't allow your tough exterior to morph into an impenetrable coat of armour. Surround yourself with people who encourage your sense of love, compassion and enjoyment. Ideally, what we need out of a friend is someone who will care about us – our life, our fears, our dreams, our successes and our failures. Someone who wants to spend time with us, someone who will listen and help us when we are struggling and someone to let loose with.

When you start with building the friendship you have with yourself, and being the kind of friend that you would want to have, you will build long-lasting friendships to be proud of.

Final Friendship Reflections

1. There is a saying that we are the sum of the five closest people to us. Consider your five closest friendships:
    - List the positive and negative aspects of each relationship (e.g. a positive could be 'known each other since three years old' and a negative might be 'attending different high schools');
    - List the strengths and weaknesses of each friend (e.g. a strength might be 'always keen to catch up' and a weakness might be 'bails at the whiff of a better offer');
    - List the strengths and weaknesses of yourself as a friend in each of the relationships you have listed (e.g. a strength might be 'always give her time to talk out her problems' and a weakness might be 'don't always defend her if other people are saying negative things about her').
2. Consider the negative points you wrote down for each friendship and the weaknesses for each friend:
    - In what ways do you think you contribute to this situation or allow it to continue?
    - List at least one constructive thing that you can do to improve the situation with each friend; OR if you think that it will never improve, list one thing you can do to protect your feelings from this person continuing to hurt you.

3. Consider how your friendships differ depending on when the friendship was started, e.g. before high school, during high school or after high school:
    - Have your friendships evolved over time?
    - Is there room for change in your relationship dynamic?
4. Consider your friendship with yourself:
    - Do you extend the same strengths to yourself as you do in your other friendships?
    - Consider some ways that you might strengthen your friendship with yourself; for instance, being kind to yourself when you make mistakes, accepting your character traits and loving yourself for the good and the bad, and acknowledging everything that you have to offer as a person.

Chapter Four
White Knight

As girls, we are often subjected to the message that in order to be saved from a solitary life of spinster-ish singleness, we need a mate to complete us. Almost every fairy tale and Hollywood movie is based on this concept. Whatever your sexual preference is, as we grow up there is constant and increasing pressure to find the person that will make us whole again, our soulmate. The one person that we have been searching for. Because in the whole wide world there is only one. And you must find this one person out of the 7.5 billion people on this planet. And thus you will be complete.

I'm quite a romantic at heart so I fell for this story, hook, line and sinker. I was an awkward teenager who lacked all self-worth so it made sense that I didn't feel enough as I was. As long as I could find someone who would have me, it would prove to the world and to me that I wasn't a complete failure at life. Not surprisingly, I found it difficult in high school to have any meaningful relationships. The initial spark of interest resulted in some blushed flirting, often without my crush even realising, but occasionally I was met with reciprocated attraction and eventual hooking-up. Even so, my relationships lacked the deeper connection that comes with emotional maturity.

That's not to say that there weren't at times genuine magnetism and a general degree of care and affection. It just so happened that my emotional barriers were impenetrable at that time, and so my relationships ended in tears, always. I ended up being both the dumper and the dumped and neither felt nice. I felt all of the feelings – the resentment after staying too long in a relationship I wanted to get out of and the subsequent anxiety about having the break-up conversation, and then the guilt after I finally summoned up the courage to call or text that I just wasn't feeling it. Alternatively, if I was dumped, there was the utter heartbreak caused by the unrequited union of true soulmates and a state of deep, depressive self-loathing following the rejection.

False starts...

My first boyfriend out of high school was a bit fucked. Let's refer to him as John. He had worked at the Fruit & Veg where I worked throughout high school. We met just as I was leaving the fruit shop to seek greener career pastures. He was a Southside boy and I was a Northside girl, so it felt like we came from completely different worlds. He and his family were devout Seventh Day Adventists and I merely posed as a Catholic at school and on certain holidays throughout the year. It was all quite intense and I felt out of my comfort zone in a lot of ways.

There was something about John. He wasn't super attractive but he was incredibly charismatic and funny and didn't care what anyone thought about him. He was spontaneous and life with him felt like an adventure. Most of all, he was super-persistent. He seemed so impressed by who I was and my independence (I had just moved out of home – he, conversely, had been kicked out of his and was living in his car). He held my life choices in a high regard and that completely had me at 'hello', given that I secretly felt lost. He called and texted me all the time. I had been particularly boyfriend-free for a while and became a bit addicted to the attention.

These were the days just prior to Tinder, Facebook and Instagram, so you literally had to get to know someone before you knew them. It wasn't as easy as half an hour of reconnaissance on social media to find out about their friends, their interests and the kind of person they were. And to be honest, I just wasn't very savvy when it came to love because I never had a whole lot of guidance, nor was I inclined to ask my parents or even my friends for advice – I never liked to admit when I didn't know something. But without realising how much I simply did not know, like what I wanted in a relationship or for my future, I was naively falling head-first into an emotional abyss.

John was a couple of years older than me and seemed to know what he wanted from a relationship. He was open about the fact that he had an ex-girlfriend whom he had dated for seven years (yes, you read that correctly – from thirteen years old to twenty years old) and they had broken up only three months earlier. Silly me, I had absolutely no idea that he was rebounding straight into my uncharted territory, and there was nothing I could do to stop myself from falling for his declaration of love. I was catching what he was pitching even if it was a foul ball.

I went along with it all, thinking that I had found someone who really *got* me. It was my first experience of being completely sucked in by desire. About six weeks of complete bliss went by, spending nights together, going to parties in suburbs I had never heard of, meeting new people and dabbling in various new substances. Before long, it seemed that the good graces of his friends had run dry and he no longer had a place to couch-surf. I said he could stay with me for the short-term, which ended up in a permanent living situation way before we were ready for it.

I felt like I was flying at the same time as drowning. After about five months of a very up-and-down life together, he started becoming withdrawn, keeping his phone on silent, leaving the room to take calls and working far longer and more irregular hours. Eventually, he revealed that he was moving out of our apartment and back to his 'real' girlfriend – the one whom he had spent seven years with and, as it turned out, had been shagging the entire time we were together. Apparently, she was the love of his life. Not me. So I did what any normal person would do, I threw all of his shit into a pile at the front door, drank an entire bottle of Wild Turkey, and considered setting his stuff alight. Didn't.

That was the first time I'd ever truly had my heart broken and I realised that just because someone looked you in the eyes and said that they loved you, they actually might not mean it. The funny thing is, when I look back at that time and deep into my heart, I can remember my own hesitation in saying, "I love you too." There was always that intuitive little voice inside me asking, "Are you sure?" I mean, I barely knew the guy.

Of course, I nursed anger, resentment and feelings of betrayal for months, even years, after the way John handled himself at the end of our relationship. But perhaps, had he not been such a cheating dead shit, my first experience with love may have turned into a super awkward situation. If he was genuine, then I would've been the bad guy. I would have had to weasel out of everything that I had promised him, like a lifetime of love and commitment. The heartbreak aside, he really did me a massive favour in the end.

It turns out that dating a loser doesn't have to be a life sentence. Hindsight gives you this glorious perspective.

What does a relationship mean to you?

- Consider your feelings about being in a relationship, remembering that you are enough, just as you are, and you don't need someone to complete you or save you.
- What do you expect from a potential partner? How do you want to be treated? What would you like to have in common with your partner?
- How you would feel within a good relationship? How you would benefit from the love that you share with your partner?
- What do you want out of a relationship?

Love, dove, glove...

It is hard to know at the time what true love really means. When you are in the midst of a new relationship, the endorphins are flowing and you start having regular sex maybe for the first time but certainly more intimately than ever before. It's an intoxicating feeling when your partner looks at you like you are an undiscovered Wonder of the World. You feel nervous about fucking it up and are unsure how to communicate your feelings without coming on too strong. You want to be good – the best they've ever had. Desire is dizzying and can be easy to mistake for true love.

It feels amazing to connect with someone, to have a new best friend who is more than just a friend. You are able to share your life and your inner world with them while staring into each other's eyes. Your partner acknowledges how special you are and you almost believe them. No one else matters as much as each other and life outside of each other's arms becomes tedious and dragging.

Other areas of our life start to be neglected. Work is uninspiring, even more so than usual. Friends just don't understand how deeply you are feeling these new feelings. No matter how much you talk about your new love, it just isn't enough. You just want to be with them. Family responsibilities take a back seat and you find yourself seeing less and less of your parents, which causes nervous advice from Mum or patronising comments from Dad. You deny that a honeymoon phase exists in your case. It's just love, plain and true.

Wide open...

Once you're all the way in, it's impossible to back out. After a while, the initial intensity begins to dwindle and suddenly Fear pops its head up to ask why you opened your heart up so widely. Sneaky insecurities start to gate-crash the party and every negative belief about yourself becomes reflected within the relationship. Painful memories of any past hurt you have experienced rise to the surface, which affects your emotions and behaviour, causing complicated and undecipherable paranoia. The threat of history repeating itself, and possible abandonment or betrayal by your love, becomes too much to bear. You push your partner away and mistakenly bottle up your feelings until you're drunk and triggered by an unlikely comment or situation to explode into a full-blown confrontation.

Love is a strong emotion, but fear can be stronger. It's inevitable that, unless you come to terms with your insecurities, you will get to the point where they will prevail and your partner will declare hurtfully that you are a *psycho bitch*. Obviously you are not a psycho, you are a delicate human who is naturally responding with fear to some kind of stimulus within the relationship. It is important to ascertain whether the stimulus is real or imaginary, and whether your response is warranted or irrational.

There is a difference between listening to your intuition, and being tricked by a 'gut feeling' that is actually the churning bile of anxious paranoia. If your partner is sneaking around and you're suspicious of them cheating on you, then maybe some calm (sober) conversation about how you feel could be helpful. If they love you and respect your feelings, then they will want to work through it with you. If they turn a rational conversation into a guilt trip about you not trusting them, then at best, they are immature, unsupportive and unwilling to help you move forward in love and trust. At worst, they may have done something that they're ashamed of and are projecting their own guilt into misdirected anger towards you.

Your partner's response aside, there is always the possibility to consider that the paranoia you are feeling that they don't love you any more, or they are interested in someone else, might really be all in your head. Check in with your own feelings – are you projecting your thoughts onto them? Now that you know this person, are you two really aligned in the way that you thought you were? Sometimes we jump straight into victim mode when really we are afraid of being the bad guy.

Listening to your heart and talking through with your partner the reality of the situation is important to be able to uncover what is at the source and move past the hurt that you are carrying.

The fact is, it's easy to play the blame game but it takes a real adult to admit their own flaws and how they are affecting the strength of the relationship. If you don't accept and acknowledge your insecurities, then it's likely that you'll bring anxiety into every relationship and continue to repeat this pattern. There is no shame in this, and it might take a few gos at a relationship to identify your own patterns and emotional bullshit. Don't limit your own growth because you are too busy trying to keep a relationship alive. If it is meant to be, then it will be. Focus on your own development and you will grow to be strong enough to give love unconditionally, and get through any relationship problems.

Love versus Fear

- How do you express your fears in your relationship? How does your partner express theirs? Do you respond to each other with love and support, or anger and hurt? What's one thing you could do to invite honest and open conversation rather than push each other away?
- What painful memories and negative beliefs perpetuate your fears?
- When have you acted upon a 'gut feeling' which later turned out to be a fear-based response or overreaction to a situation? Is there a time in a relationship when you wish you had listened to your intuition?

Soulmates...

For me, my first real love after the false start I spoke about earlier, in which I actually fell into real mutual love, was with a shy and sweet guy named Adam, who showed me great respect and loved me wholeheartedly.

We had a long and intense honeymoon period, extended by the fact that I had lived a couple of hours' drive away from him for the first six months of our relationship and we were both nursing some raw wounds from previous respective relationships. We had a lot in common at the time and cared deeply for each other, looked after one another and had fun together.

It was about eighteen months to two years into our romance that the first cracks began to show. As we grew up, our interests changed and we evolved into adults that suddenly weren't so similar. We denied the cracks and covered them up for as long as we could with our genuine love for each other and our obsession with the idea that we were 'meant to be'. It wasn't all bad but it certainly was hard work. The niggly problems turned into full-blown battles and after some long years together, it got to a point where the drama was constant and we were either in a state of bliss or total disarray.

After a few years together, I was ultimately unhappy with how Adam treated me and the way he would still abandon me for his friends all of the time. We had completely separate social lives and interests. It didn't feel like he was invested in me as a person but instead he had this idea of who he wanted and would project that onto me (i.e. a housewife). Our fights consisted of me threatening to break it off in an attempt to change the way things were, as opposed to actually ending the relationship. He would stop me from leaving by saying all of the things I wanted to hear.

As Adam tried to prove his love for me with words, I tried to tell myself that I could believe him, that it would get better. I would be bitterly disappointed when his actions did not match his pleas for more chances. He seemed genuine in terms of wanting to change but nothing ever did. I never even considered whether we wanted the same things. Adam was dead set on marriage and babies and I wasn't sure about those things, especially because we weren't even enjoying each other's company on a basic level any more. I was uncertain about how we could face such life challenges together and still emerge happy and whole.

But how could I resist a guy that wanted to commit to me like that? For real love, you try hard. You accept that there will be flaws in the relationship. Nothing's perfect, right? Even if we fought incessantly, we made up eventually. I could see that neither of us was blameless – he hurt me with his actions and then I hurt him back with my words. We continued on and made it work as best we could. But it was exhausting. And so we reached an inevitable breaking point.

It's really difficult to break up with someone when you once thought that they were the one true love of your life. Your heart feels as if it has been ripped, still beating, out of your chest. However, inside yourself you reach a point where you just can't keep dealing with the differences. It comes down to values and what is important to you. It also comes down to how you are willing to be treated within a relationship.

Relationship Reflections

- What understanding about romantic relationships do you have from childhood? Consider the relationship of your parents/guardians. What example of love has been set for you? Perhaps they had a strong marriage that equated to a tight-knit family. Perhaps the conventional values of marriage were there but it seemed strained or loveless. Maybe your parents split up but they were able to have a second chance at love. Maybe you were raised by a single parent–consider their attitude towards love and relationships.
- How does the example of those close to you in your life affect your own feelings about love and relationships? In what ways do you aspire to be similar and/or different?
- Did you have a similar upbringing to your partner? Do you have the same values? Are the things that are most important to you in life also the most important to them as well? Do you see the world in the same way? For example, 'Life is an exciting opportunity', 'The world is a cruel place or somewhere you don't belong'.

The beginning of the end...

When you finally end it, you are left to percolate in your own pain, alone. If you have alienated yourself by having less contact with your friends and family during the intense early stages of your relationship, then you feel very alone indeed. All you can think about is lying in bed with your ex and looking at their face. You miss being held and comforted and having someone to talk to. It's like a double-hit because you are not only suffering significant agony, you don't have your closest ally any more to tell you that everything is going to be okay.

You are forced to distance yourself from your ex's family so that you can finally move on from the drama. But that doesn't stop you from sadly texting his mum to say thanks for everything. You block your ex on Facebook but you still torture yourself by catching up with his sister every second Tuesday so that you can hear the latest news about his life (yes, yes, you're *friends*…). It's heart breaking to hear that he is still going out with his mates like normal.

If you are anything like me, it might take a few break-ups within the same relationship to really get the picture that it's over. Adam and I broke up the first time after being together for two-and-a-half years, and we had a break for about three months. During this time, I still had a key to his house, so there were a few instances where I would just show up drunk in the middle of the night and find my way into his bed (luckily, he never had anyone else in there). We really felt like we needed each other in this desperate way. Like we completed each other.

When we both woke up in the light of day with our immediate urges fulfilled, there was still the big gaping hole inside ourselves that we couldn't seem to satisfy for each other. Even so, we thought it would be a good idea to try again, to make a real go of it this time. There had to be a reason why we couldn't get over each other, we must be soulmates after all.

Adam bought me a pair of diamond earrings as a display of his commitment, which underwhelmed me to be honest (I have never been a 'things' person – I would have preferred he spent the thousands of dollars on airfares for a holiday to spend together instead but, case in point, our different desires from life). Even so, without wanting to seem like an ungrateful bitch, I settled for the fact he was declaring I was special and he was willing to make it work. Regardless of the previous heartache, if there had been a diamond for my ring finger, then I probably would have said yes, such was my ignorance to the actual significance of this and my resolute commitment to our love.

Eventually, after almost four years of broken promises, hurtful comments about each other, and my self-esteem largely destroyed, the love had officially drained away until we were both too empty to continue. My exhaustion from fighting trumped my fear of being alone forever. We tearfully called it quits for good.

When my relationship with Adam was finally and definitely over for real, it was a relief but also an empty feeling. Where did all of the love go? At one point in my life, this person was the most important part of my own existence, and then, all of a sudden, it's done. Over. It felt like a complete waste of time and emotional energy after ending so prematurely. What had I been fighting for? It was an anti-climax of the greatest proportions. I suddenly felt hollow because the drama had disappeared from my daily life and all I had left to focus on was my uncertain future.

Am I dating my dad?

After a few weeks of hysterical weeping at inopportune times, I tried to reflect but I couldn't get past the blame. It was my default position to see Adam as the person who ruined us because he wasn't good enough and wouldn't change. I wore my pain like a badge of honour, as if to show everyone how much I had been put through, how much I'd had to withstand and what a survivor I was. I was also melting down about the thought of being alone forever, although I was only twenty-three. I felt like my one great opportunity at love had passed, and now I was destined to have cats.

Time went on and I remained stuck in the emotional funk of an angry little victim. I had completely exhausted my friends' ears so I needed a new listener who wouldn't judge my deepest and darkest fears. My mum finally sat me down and suggested I see a psychologist to talk it out. At twenty-three years old, I never even considered that I wouldn't be able to figure something out on my own. But it turned out that the psychologist was easy to connect with, a middle-aged woman who surely knew a thing or two about the pain and torture of love. She started off the sessions by asking me about my childhood and my relationship with my parents, mostly my father. I was confused because I thought we were there to talk about my ex-boyfriend. But she explained that she preferred to start with early background so she could get an idea of who I was. Sounded reasonable.

After talking about my dad and my relationship with him, she then asked me to open up about my relationship with Adam. It was uncanny how the same words kept repeating themselves. Emotionally unavailable. Self-absorbed. Physically absent. I felt abandoned by my dad when he left when I was nine years old, and I felt abandoned by Adam every time he chose his friends over me. The similarities in the relationship pattern were extensive. And, yes, I was completely confused and grossed out by the thought that I'd chosen someone who was similar to my dad.

This massive realisation pushed me to appreciate that there was more going on in my mind and my heart than I was letting myself accept and process. It was the first time I ever took responsibility for my own actions within the relationship, and had a broader understanding of why I was so desperate to change my ex-boyfriend into the 'potential' that I thought he could be. I was repeating this dynamic because it was the only way I knew how to be with a man. Weird but true. I may have even been subconsciously trying to heal my relationship with my dad through Adam.

No matter how great our upbringing, we all have baggage from times in our life where we have been hurt or have felt like we've been mistreated. It's common for us to seek out our first partner or major relationship to mirror a relationship that we've already had, even if it is dysfunctional, because it feels safer. I know it sounds gross but, yes, you may try to repeat a relationship dynamic that you've had with your father or mother. It's like, better the devil you know than the devil you don't.

Maybe your mother was an alcoholic and you tend to migrate towards friends and partners who have issues with substance abuse or need 'helping' or 'fixing' in some way. Maybe your dad left your family when you were young or he was emotionally absent, and you find yourself in relationships where you are constantly seeking approval, attention and the feeling of being 'looked after'. Sometimes this pattern isn't always negative – you might subconsciously aim for a relationship that mirrors the love of your parents' relationship.

Acceptance of my own version of this pattern instantly brought it into my conscious mind and made it a situation that could never be repeated again, and also helped me to heal old wounds with my dad as well.

Loving someone unconditionally versus loving someone's potential...

Another poignant lesson I figured out during my reflections with the psychologist was that we can never actually be with someone's 'potential'. We have to love our partner as they are, without needing to change them. If you find yourself saying, "They are the perfect partner except for..." or "We could be so happy, if only he would just...," then you are not loving your partner unconditionally for who they are right now. Even if they are telling you that they want to change this part of themselves, if they are not actively working on self-improvement then it's just lip service and you are both contributing to the ultimate breakdown of your relationship.

And, remember, if the two of you want different things from life, this person just might not be the right person. It doesn't mean that the love isn't real.

Love can be fierce and genuine, and also a complete waste when two people are fighting to get to their own different end points.

The only thing you can do is work on who you are and identify what you want, so that you can truly know whether the person that you love is going to walk beside you through life.

Moving on...

Instead of pushing Adam to be someone different, I needed to focus on healing my own insecurities by acknowledging and accepting the pain that I had experienced in my earlier life, and my personality traits that had become destructive. Only then could I be in touch with my true needs and attract a partner into my life that would fulfil my real idea of love. I put my energy into moving forward as a person which empowered me to focus on the lessons I had learned. It wasn't all motivational quotes and inspired thinking but I got over the Facebook stalking pretty quickly (it hurts too much) and made a conscious effort to let go, even in situations where others tried to force me to revisit the drama.

Your Relationships…

- Consider your first significant relationship. What were the issues that caused the ultimate demise? Who was responsible for what action or behaviour? Try to consider yourself an equal player in the relationship, even if you were the victim of cheating or game-playing (excluding any form of actual abuse, obviously).
- If you are still in your first significant relationship, what is the dynamic like in the partnership? Consider the balance of power and who holds the most cards. What issues do you have that keep popping up? Is it an issue that you can put up with for life, or are you relying on your partner to change a part of themselves? Are they willing or able to do that? In what ways are you holding on to their 'potential'?
- How do you contribute to the issues in your relationship? For example, do you have the tendency to be jealous or do you remain passive about problems until you reach breaking point? Do you try to get his friends/family on your side of the argument because you need to be right all of the time? It's okay to admit these things to yourself– remember that they are a form of self-sabotage and acceptance and acknowledgement are the key to growth.
- Where in your childhood could these patterns and habits stem from? Are you still unconsciously struggling to be seen or heard, or is this a learned behaviour from a difficult time in your life?

I planned to be single for a while after Adam, to really reinforce my own strength as a woman, and continue to learn what I wanted from this life, outside of the comfort zone of a relationship.

I was spurred into a golden few months of post-psychologist personal development. Not to mention that my bestie had moved into my house when Adam moved out, so it felt as if good times were ahead. And then, God help me, I fell in love again.

Life always has mysterious and unexpected plans for us...

I'd known Mitch since I was eighteen and had always had a soft spot for his energy and sense of humour but never had considered his potential as anything more in my life. One fateful weekend he texted me to say hi, and the next thing I knew we were meeting up with our mutual friends, drinking, laughing, dancing, kissing and then going home together… We were magnetised to each other's energy. Suddenly we were a 'thing' and it took everyone by surprise, including us.

Adam and I had been over for five months but it felt so soon to be starting something new. I wasn't sure if I was ready, and still harboured a lot of insecurities and trust issues. In the beginning, Mitch and I took things slowly but it had started to sink in early on for both of us that these feelings weren't going anywhere. The more we got to know each other, the more we realised just how much our values, our interests and the way we saw the world were similar. Mostly, we cruised through our first year together with natural ease and sense of fun, with only the occasional drunken argument.

I'm incredibly grateful that Mitch never mollycoddled me or indulged my insecurities because I had been hurt in a relationship before. While he is a compassionate person, he was very upfront about the fact that he didn't want to be compared to any previous love of mine. I was forced out of the old relationship dynamic I had become accustomed to, in order to grow as a person within this new relationship. I sacrificed the part of myself that felt comfortable as the small, submissive, victimised person I used to be, and became strong, equal and emotionally fulfilled, the way Mitch also expected me to be. He was raised by a strong, confident and optimistic woman and his respect for my strength as an individual helped me immensely to become fiercely independent, and therefore more equipped to love.

Mitch and I have been together since 2010 and we continue to grow and change as people, and yet continue to love and support each other. We may have disagreements and occasionally hurt each other's feelings but we humbly apologise (eventually) and genuinely move on. Nothing is perfect but there's no more drama, no more games. He wants me to succeed in my dreams and vice versa – we work on them together. Each day that we spend together is a choice and not a necessity. We consciously choose each other with every word and every action, and we know that we are each other's first priority but not only priority. It's a refreshing kind of love, a love without fear.

All the single ladies...

It may not always feel like it but it really is okay to be alone, too. Looking back, I wish I had possessed the inner resources and strength to allow myself to be single for longer periods of time. In between my more significant relationships, I filled up many months with meaningless hook-ups because I was instantly lonely in my own company. And these were not the empowered kind of romantic liaisons. I hate to think of myself at that time as desperate, but I would be severely disappointed if I went home alone to face an empty bed and an aching heart.

Even if you are less tragic than I was, being single can bring up just as much insecurity as being in a relationship, just in a different way. If your solitary routine becomes a safe zone, then you can become your own worst enemy when you're single. It's a wonderful opportunity to use your independence to discover who you are and to be okay with that. Continue to be strong but also stay open.

Understand that loving yourself also involves inviting in and accepting love from others as well, otherwise you risk closing yourself off from true connection through vulnerability and intimacy.

Thought patterns in relationships

Whether you are single or in a relationship, each of us carries with us patterns of thought and behaviour that affect our relationship dynamics, based on our upbringing, self-esteem and life experiences. For the process of growth and becoming stronger within yourself in order to give love fully and without fear, it's essential to acknowledge your own patterns of thought and behaviour and then reframe them to a more supportive mindset.

Consider negative thought patterns that pop up in your mind when you are having issues in your relationship or you are feeling bad about not being in a relationship.

For example, a negative thought pattern that used to come up for me often was that I would be cheated on by my partner, confirming that my inner fear of being worthless was correct, that no one was to be trusted with my love, and that the hurtful actions of others were always out of control, making me a weak, dependent sitting-duck.

To reframe this unhelpful thought process which was essentially sabotaging my relationships, I developed affirmations which powerfully broke through the unconscious pattern and built up my ability to know what I deserved and what I expected from a relationship.

I deserve to be happy and loved.
My worth is not dictated by the actions of others.
It is safe to trust that others will do the right thing by me.
If my partner treats me unacceptably, I trust that I will be strong enough to take action in my own best interest.

Develop your own affirmations relevant to your negative internal thought process. For the most powerful impact, say these daily while looking yourself in the eye in the mirror.

If you have been single for a long time, be careful not to let your soft interior be completely overwhelmed by a tough, impenetrable outer shell. Protect yourself, not just from the unknown of relationships, but also from yourself.

The beauty of love lies not only in the pleasure of the first stages of lust, desire and excitement but also in the pain of the mistakes, and the small moments between getting to know someone inside and out. Experiencing love is arguably the point of life, but hurt will inevitably come along for the ride. In love, in fear and in pain, you will always learn something about yourself.

Chapter Five
Layers of the Onion

Navigating high school and the few of years after that is like being in a bad dream where you are taking a dip in the muddy waters of the Amazon River while trying to dodge the piranhas that want to eat your flesh. But then you look down and realise that the piranhas lived inside you all along and, bite after bite, they are slowly reducing you to a slush of chummy fish food.

You go through life suspicious that everyone else is out to get you but really it's your own active self-hatred that does the most damage.

We tend to place our own happiness in the hands of others by letting their opinion of us dictate how we feel about ourselves. Everyone is better, cooler, knows more than us, but they are also the enemy. We get close but not close enough that we let our guard down. Inside we berate ourselves for looking the way we do, not being funnier, not having experienced as much as everyone else. Without realising it, we become our own worst enemy, keeping our real selves distanced from our friends so that they can't see how secretly pathetic we are. We hate the person that we are. We refuse to look at ourselves in the mirror other than to slather on our daily mask.

But how can we hate someone that we refuse to get to know?

During high school and the couple of years afterwards, I never cared to know who I was, because I was always trying to be someone else. Someone a little cooler or wilder, more funny and interesting. I had different versions of myself that I would show the world at my own discretion – Caring Friend Laura, Let's Get Drunk and Dance Laura, and then Confused, Depressed Laura, who was mostly a secret, unless I felt neglected and needed sympathy and attention to feel better. No one knew the whole me, the real me, not even me. This got pretty exhausting and I ended up resenting most people for not taking the time to understand me, even though I never gave them the opportunity.

Sure, my friends weren't perfect and played the occasional mind game to make themselves feel good. At the end of the day, they had their own dramas and insecurities and were still figuring out their own relationship with themselves and others. Mostly we all had the same needs. Mostly they just wanted to be there for me, to have fun with me and enjoy my company, and vice versa. But I struggled to let them in. I perpetuated the cycle of sadness and confusion by responding with a toughened exterior to protect that secret, vulnerable part of me. Coming out of my self-constructed shell took a lot of conscious effort but I realised that I was holding myself back from real connections with people.

As time passed and I muddled my way through my late-teens and early-twenties, I had a lot of experiences that helped me realise who I was not. Failed relationships, jobs and career paths that didn't feel good and inevitably didn't work out, friendships with toxic dynamics that had to be let go. Many painful and difficult experiences that made life feel messy and confusing.

Every step of the way, I resisted change, I resisted growth, I tried to be tough and strong and keep my head in the sand about anything that caused too much exposure of my raw inner self. She was a person that I just did not care to get close to. She wasn't worth it, and I thought it much easier to pretend I was someone else. Meanwhile, as my friends continued to get to know themselves, they seemed more and more at ease while I floundered. I strived to be cooler and faked confidence to fit in with the dominant personalities in my group.

The awkward, messy, uncomfortable times never really had a clear end point, but did eventually streamline to become more functional and less dramatic. I reached a comfortable, yet grim and begrudging flow where life just continued on. After some years of living out of home, I had a certain sense of independence, even if a little empty and lonely. I focused on my strengths at work and kept going to a job that I was good at even if it left me unfulfilled. The more manipulative and draining friendships became less central to my social life and I strengthened my bond over time with more genuine and aligned friends. I cooled off my internal fight enough to stop actively hating myself, still disconnected and indifferent yet less angry and resentful.

Life was okay, but unexceptional...

You never really know that there is more work to be done, until you're thrown into a situation where you are forced to re-evaluate everything. In my mid-twenties, my relationship with Adam had ended and I was feeling empty and lonely. We had decided to buy a house together in a last ditch bid to be 'serious', so I was financially stretched and living there alone. Each night I spent percolating in buyer's remorse, feelings of being trapped in a nightmare of my own making and the regret of failure and missed opportunity.

I was also miserable in my professional career. Nothing was wrong with my job; in fact, I was earning pretty good money but I had tired of the subtle sexism of the corporate environment and the daily grind of pasting on a smile and performing like a monkey. I felt like I needed to relinquish my original life plan and take back control of my life. I was sick of being an assistant, regardless of my trumped-up executive title and had no desire to keep playing the game and climbing the ladder. My soul was calling me to stop settling and do something more meaningful, marking the real beginning of my inner journey.

Over the next few years, I started a degree qualification in naturopathy and a diploma in counselling. I began to learn about my body and consider my life and my influences from the very beginning. I started to realise something that should be common sense but had never occurred to me – without understanding what was going on inside myself, physically, psychologically and emotionally, I could never understand the world or find my place within it. I was ignoring my point of view because I didn't believe I was important, but I was stuck in limbo, not having a voice, and not moving forward.

Healing required confrontation. Growth required acknowledgement.

After years of working in an office setting, I thought about most of the people I worked with, and they were clearly unhealthy and unfulfilled. I didn't want to end up that way, and I knew that lifestyle didn't suit me. The strength and determination to change couldn't possibly be more challenging than the strength required to stay in the same draining mindset. Listening to my inner voice uncovered inexplicable insight to my fears and my dreams. I found the thought of helping other people do the same very appealing, to lift the burden of weight from others' shoulders, like I had done for myself.

This realisation started out as only a curious little niggle in the beginning but eventually turned into an epiphany of life-changing proportions. The self-discovery process over the subsequent years of study and work with health practitioners was a mixed bag of self-validation, joy, shame, awkwardness and anxiety. I delved deeply into my past, my relationship with myself and others, my upbringing, my personal triumphs and embarrassments.

I was slowly becoming who I always was, integrating all of the parts of myself into one piece.

Your own process might look completely different, more subtle or more drawn out. Your emotional breakthrough might present over time or after a major life change, like a break-up or loss of job. Or you might just wake up one day and decide that you need to change – just like that. Either way, personal growth will inevitably find you, whether you welcome it or not. On the surface, it can look like complete self-destruction but it's more like a seed breaking apart to create the flower, or an egg cracking from the inside to make way for the chick.

I have reflected a great deal on this period in my life and wondered why I first had to be everything that I didn't want to be in order to discover myself in such a laboured way. Growing up, I was taught to soldier on through whatever circumstances were present in life – sickness, boredom, sadness – so I never really stopped to question myself, my thoughts, my reactions or my beliefs. It was impossible for me to learn these lessons any earlier because I simply was not receptive to changing my thinking.

Life provides a steady stream of events which, in hindsight, plays out in perfect timing but I'd be lying if I said it wasn't frustrating to look back at the long, uncomfortable years of developing my relationship with myself. If things had been different, would I have had the strength to be kinder to myself, to let go of my internal suffering and pain, and see things as they really were? Would I have been so scared to be myself or would I have embraced my differences? Could I have let my real light shine and inspired others to be their unique self as well?

The hardest part of growing up is learning to be yourself, to accept all of the different parts of yourself and even, dare I say, grow to like them. All of the features of your face, your freckles, the lumps and bumps of your body, the pockmarks, the stretch marks, the cellulite and the saggy boobs. Your stubbornness, lack of direction, procrastination and insecurities. It would be a sad waste of a life to let these characteristics stop you from living, laughing and loving.

In hindsight, everyone feels the same spectrum of 'shitness' throughout this stage of life. Of course, there are good times too, but anyone who is projecting nothing but love and light is either lying to you or to themselves. The act is exhausting and they will inevitably break character. If I could travel back and have a conversation with my twenty-year-old self, I wouldn't try to change the course of events but simply tell her that she is loved and she is enough, just as she is. I would tell her to believe in herself and all she has to offer. And I would tell her to stay hopeful, because the future holds more goodness than she could possibly imagine.

Knowing yourself = loving yourself

Understanding yourself is the key to realising where you fit into the world and can help you tune in to what is important to you. It allows you to really recognise who you are and where your purpose in this life lies. It can help you to build successful friendships and relationships, to choose career paths that will suit your personality and purpose, to find meaning in your existence, and to help you feel valued and of worth, to others and to yourself.

Getting to know yourself is a commitment and a lifelong process of learning acceptance, compassion and flexibility. The following exercises are a little more in depth than other chapters but were essential tools for me to gain a proper understanding of my layers of thinking and my belief patterns deeply rooted in my psyche.

Exercises to Get to Know Yourself

1. Personality Types

Introversion and Extroversion

If you are unsure of the meaning of introversion and extroversion, or under which banner you fit, this is an easy and informative place to start to understand your personality and how you relate to other people.

Growing up, I was very much an introverted character type, which meant I was comfortable in my own company and had the tendency to be a bit of a wallflower in a group. I wish I'd known back then that I wasn't an alienated loner or had problems connecting with people because I had nothing to offer. The reality was that I found shallow interaction like small talk to be excruciating. I thought at the time that I should be more outgoing and enjoy being the centre of attention but that just wasn't me. As I have become more confident in myself, I am much more easy-going in groups but I still prefer one-on-one conversations that are meaningful, than competing for attention in a large group. I enjoy socialising but tend to retreat and recharge my batteries with alone time.

How about you? Understanding whether you are introverted or extroverted, or where you fit on the spectrum between the two, can bring to light your personality strengths and weaknesses, the environment in which you will thrive and how you relate to other people.

Myers Briggs

Taking this concept a step further is the Myers Briggs personality test. If you Google Myers Briggs, then you will find many online quizzes that you can take, and you will receive a score of four letters. I personally am an INFJ, which stands for 'Introverted iNtuitive Feeling Judging'. There are sixteen personality combinations and the result can give excellent insight into who you are and what drives you. It also outlines suggested career paths based on your personality characteristics. Like anything of this nature, it may not be completely accurate as we are all complex individuals but it may form a basis for developing your ideas and inspiration about the essence of who you are.

2. Values

Our values define what we value in this world, so by understanding our values we get a sense of what is most important to us in our lives. This will change as we age and our priorities shift but thinking through our values regularly can help ensure that we're making choices defined by what motivates us. We can also make sure that our partners want the same things, because this is so important to keeping a relationship together for the long-term. It sounds basic but identifying what you really want sets you down a clear path that is expressive of your uniqueness. Even if the path changes course, it is better than blindly stumbling through life, acquiring things instead of meaning.

Draw up a table like the one below and outline ten to twenty values. You don't have to order them straight away – just start listing things that are important to you. For example, this might mean spending time with family and possibly creating a family of your own one day. Maybe you love to travel, and so you want your life to revolve around this. Career, friendships and love will no doubt appear somewhere on the list.

Once you have listed ten to twenty areas of value, you can rank them in the order of priority that they mean to you and give them a score which shows how satisfied you currently are with that component of your life. You'll then easily be able to identify which parts of yourself or areas of your life that you want to build on because they are the most important to you.

Rank in Priority / Order	Value and Description	Current level of satisfaction (Out of 10)

3. Strengths and Weaknesses

In order to discover your strengths, write down everything you love and adapt these into personal characteristics. For example, if you love to cook for others, you might have a loving and generous spirit. If you love being with friends, it could be that you enjoy socialising and being a source of support.

In order to discover your weaknesses, think about the things that drain you or fill you with dread and these may help you to understand your weaknesses. These are not necessarily judgements on what is 'bad' about you but should focus on skills you would like to develop. For instance, you may hate public speaking, so shyness may be a current weakness.

When it comes to strengths and weaknesses, it is also essential to identify the ways in which you sabotage yourself, and stop yourself from expressing your strengths. The ways in which we self-sabotage are forms of weakness because they expose our deepest insecurities and fears. Some forms of self-sabotage may include procrastination, fear of failure, fear of success, comparison to others, over-thinking, indecision, holding onto a victim mentality and blaming others. Consider all that may apply to you and the circumstances in which you self-sabotage the most.

4. Layers of the Psyche

I'm sure you have an idea in your mind about the old-school psychotherapist, Sigmund Freud – the stern expression, the white hair, the accent. 'Lie down on the couch and tell me about your childhood…'

Therapy doesn't really work like that anymore but the guy had some pretty revolutionary ideas. Freud's theories have been picked apart and argued to death over the years and there may be modern psychoanalytic theories; however, Freud's understanding of the different layers within the psyche were a practical way to identify thought patterns and processes which resonate with me.

Freud said that there is a constant balancing act between the three layers of the psyche – Id, Ego and Superego – which impacts your thoughts, feelings and behaviours. Knowing the parts of your conscious and unconscious mind, you can move towards recognising what part of your brain is dictating your choices and actions.

According to Freud:

The Id – The unconscious, instinctive and primitive component of the brain that is driven by the pleasure principle. The Id strives for immediate gratification of all desires, and if this does not occur then tension, anxiety or stress can quickly erupt. The Id is very important in the first few years of life because it ensures a baby's needs are met. However, if the Id continues to dictate actions and behaviour, then as an older child or adult, it becomes socially unacceptable and disruptive. The Id has no concept of morality so it can equate to ugly adult tantrums, addictive behaviour, or acting without considering the consequences.

The Ego – The Ego is the middle ground which consciously develops from the Id. It ensures impulses can be expressed in a socially acceptable manner in the real world and allows us to negotiate with our impulsive desires through delaying gratification to eventual satisfaction. Like craving bad food but waiting until the weekend to eat it. The Ego makes sure we act like adults with appropriate reactions and rational thinking.

The Superego – This is the last component of the personality to develop and contains all of the ideals that we inherit from our parents and society, our moral standards for good and bad, right and wrong. The feelings we get from abiding by our personal moral code may be those of pride for good behaviour or guilt for bad behaviour. It is our Superego that imposes all judgement and attempts to perfect and civilise our actions by employing our self-critical inner voice to try and live up to an ideal instead of a realistic standard.

If you have a strong sense of Ego, a realistic outlook not governed by your Id or your Superego, then you may function normally and be generally in control of your actions. Conflict arises when the Ego loses out to the urges of the Id or the perfectionistic tendencies of the Superego. Be aware of these three aspects and recognise when imbalance occurs; for instance, the Id dictating unhealthy fulfilment of impulses such as overeating, overspending, gambling, drinking and drug-taking. Or the inclination of a dominant Superego to go by the book or be extremely rigid or moralistic.

Understanding these layers of the psyche helps you to know which part of your brain is most often making decisions and dictating your behaviour, and whether identification and change is necessary.

5. Inner Child and Stages of Development

Your experiences throughout childhood do not have to define you but they can affect who you are as you become an adult. Bad memories and trauma affect your feelings about yourself and the way you relate to others and the world. The child that we were unconsciously stays with us forever.

If you have experienced trauma in your childhood, or you have overwhelming feelings of danger when it comes to any form of change in your life, it's very possible that your inner child may need some extra care and attention, in order to provide more resilience to your adult self and allow trusting relationships to build throughout your adult life. There are numerous published theories that failure to complete a stage of development due to trauma at a particular age may impact skills as an adolescent or adult.

If you have suffered from terrible life events or you feel like you are particularly stuck in life and things are not moving forward, there may be some work to be done around strengthening your inner child. I recommend doing some reading and finding a counsellor or psychologist to talk to. I do not suggest attempting to delve into traumatic events on your own as this can dredge up significant emotions and memories, causing more pain than personal development.

6. Your Love Language

Love Languages are an amazing concept that was created by psychotherapist Gary Chapman, who wrote the book *The Five Love Languages*. Knowing your own Love Language can be such a vital tool in understanding how you personally express love and how you relate to your partner after the honeymoon period wears off, encouraging a deeper level of understanding and communication.

The five Love Languages are Quality Time, Words of Affirmation, Gifts, Acts of Service, and Physical Touch. Gary runs an excellent website where you can take a quiz to find out your Love Language. Knowing and understanding your subconscious expectations of love and partnership means that you can build a stronger relationship with your partner and gain a better understanding of who you are, and how to communicate your expectations.

www.5lovelanguages.com

7. Other Tools

There are endless tools in the big wide world that can help you to continue getting to know yourself. You could see an astrologist and have a complete reading using the date and time of your birth. Numerology may give insight about your personality and destined path using your personal significant numbers. You could see a counsellor, a life coach, an iridologist, a tarot reader, a psychic, a hypnotherapist… If you are being called to connect with yourself further and to uncover the secrets of your soul, then listen to this internal need. The options for development are truly endless.

Some of these things cost money, so of course you must work within your personal means. Consider this next time you want to spend a couple of hundred on a new dress or shoes that you may only wear once or not at all. The value of personal development cannot be understated and is well worth the expense if you are willing to forgo the time, energy and vulnerability to make it something special.

It's a journey, within a journey. Take your time with it. Move softly. Invest where you can. Good luck.

Chapter Six

How Not to Be a People Pleaser

There is a subtle set of underlying and poorly-defined rules for the way we should act and think if we want to be considered 'normal'. They're not actually written down anywhere but through a process of trial and error, we get to know them. This is otherwise known as social conditioning.

At a point in our lives, when it's hard enough trying to figure out who you are, let alone what you think, it takes things to another complicated level when you are also trying to work out how to present yourself to the outside world. Don't be too strong, otherwise you're aggressive. Too emotional, a sook. Too passionate, a nerd. Too funny, you're the joke. Too mature, you're a know-it-all. Too immature, you know nothing. For God's sake, don't wear your heart on your sleeve, honesty is *very uncomfortable*. Just be cool.

The issue is, there is no instruction manual to guide you on how best to be cool, and what you actually need to do to feel less emotion and how to make it seem natural. You can't possibly ask anyone how to act in order to be more likeable and attractive. Admitting to any vulnerability at all is undignified and makes your weaknesses as obvious as a pimple on the tip of your nose. There's always the looming threat that if someone knows your flaws, they may use them against you.

It is much easier for most people to sit on a fence, stay protected by a hard exterior mask and focus on the business of shallow, surface bullshit. They are only acting how they have been taught to by their parents and society. By sticking their head in the sand, it becomes easier to focus on things that may seem important – money, status, accumulation of possessions, what other people are doing – and deny any realness that might be uncomfortably accumulating under their skin.

It's a lonely feeling when you feel forced to fit in with the thoughts, opinions and actions of other people. It might feel unnatural or out of alignment with who you really are. When you begin to notice where this is happening in your life, you can realise the importance and validity of your own point of view, and sticking to it helps you define yourself and ultimately find where you fit in this world.

In the age of information, where we are constantly connected to people both in person and online, it is impossible to avoid being subjected to the influence of others. Friendships, family, cultural or religious groups and your professional network all potentially involve people who hold the expectation that you will play your part and fit into the dynamic of the group. These kinds of circles can be a valuable part of who you are and contribute to your sense of connection, community and self-worth. However, if you are still figuring out who you are, you may be vulnerable to the influence of others. This opens up potential opportunity to feel misunderstood by the people around you, leading to emptiness, dissatisfaction and regret.

As a child, the opinions of our teachers and our parents begin to shape our understanding of the world. We have permission to live in a bubble – there are things about the world that we are just too young to understand so it's essential for our safety and development that we trust our parents' judgement. Depending on your upbringing, you may have been encouraged to figure things out for yourself, go with the flow of general opinion, or you have some pretty strong views passed down from whoever raised you. My parents are pretty matter-of-fact people and never made up stories to shelter me from uncomfortable realities. However, if something was complicated or required an in-depth conversation, especially about feelings or relationships, it was usually put in the 'too hard' basket and not discussed.

My mum always encouraged me to think my own thoughts but sidestepped the part about how to deal with other people influencing the way I thought, and how I should counteract that with my own common sense. I was easily swayed by other people and it was difficult to stand up for myself or give my opinion about what I thought was right. I parroted words, phrases and opinions from my friends, and was rarely pulled up by my mother about the utter inaccuracy of my attitude, even when she didn't agree. She would just smirk and snort, knowing that I would eventually figure it out.

I took this as a display of cluelessness on my mum's behalf, cementing how much more I knew about Things than she did. I also found it frustrating when I didn't get the answers or support that I was craving. There was no Google back then. The strong values that had been instilled in me, like being honest, working hard and doing the right thing, felt like optional extras. This added to my sense of confusion and the feeling that I had to figure things out on my own.

Early development of opinions...

Think back to when you were growing up, and how free you were to express your opinions:

- How strong were the opinions of your teachers/parents?
- How does it feel now when someone you care about disagrees with you on something important?

When you're no longer a child...

Things can get really complicated if your parents want to be involved in your personal choices once you are an adult. When you are young, you have everyone weighing in on how they think your life should go and, because you are still figuring out what you want to do, it can be easier to take the advice that seems the most reasonable and productive, like taking a certain career path. Our parents have often sacrificed a lot for us and sometimes they won't let us forget it. Following their advice is considered due payment for them birthing and raising us.

Maybe your parents have never been prouder that you finally got into law, or you achieved a promotion in your fifty-hour-a-week job. At one point, you thought you wanted this life but all of a sudden your soul is calling you to travel, start your own business or seek work that helps people. And you have a big decision to make. Do you put your own plans on hold to please your parents and thereby fulfil their wishes, or do you take the immediate plunge into what your heart is telling you?

Our parents were part of a different generation where they found a job, stayed there for thirty years and worked their way up the food chain as much as possible. There was immense pride and integrity in being able to provide for your family. This was certainly an honourable way to live, no doubt about that. It showed integrity, responsibility, accountability, reliability and consistency – character qualities that we could all strive for more.

Handling parental confrontation...

If you find yourself in a situation where you need to stand your ground, be an adult. Don't stamp your feet and yell, "But I don't WANT to!" Arm yourself with the information you need to present your point of view. Ask advice from people who can provide an unbiased opinion and guide you towards a middle ground.

Although, it's important to consider the ways that times have changed, and the increasing opportunities in our modern world. Education is broader, information is easier to obtain, and travel is cheaper and faster. Going down a career path that doesn't interest you in order to please your parents may lead to persevering with a miserable life. You were not put on this planet to pay the bills. You were also not put on this planet to repeat, or to make up for, your parents' mistakes. And yet, it may be bloody hard to say no to your parents, depending on your upbringing and your cultural beliefs. Your relationship with your parents can be one of the most significant and influential factors when it comes to your choices.

If your parents are trying to push you into studying something that doesn't interest you, seek advice from the university admissions department or a course advisor on the actual parameters of the course and the post-graduate opportunities, to understand why your parents want this path for you. Usually they just want what is best for you and your future, even if it is a misguided opinion or a projection of their own personal unfulfilled dream. Bring alternatives to the table and give legitimate reasons for your lack of passion for their suggestion.

If travel is in your sights, talk to someone in their twenties who has done a gap year overseas and gain insight into what was successful for them and what they would do differently if they could do it again. Be realistic about how you might fund your adventure. Even if your parents have the money to give to you, earning enough to travel independently will show them that you are serious about doing this as a positive life step. Start thinking and planning like an adult and be assertive to get what you want.

Maybe you have no idea what your next step is. I certainly didn't have the faintest inkling of what I would be good at or even enjoy, aside from sunbathing and drinking clear spirits. I was too fearful of the future to think radically so I started by responsibly looking at realistic jobs for my age group and experience. If you want to go down the path of working, explain to your parents what qualities and characteristics you want to build before you make major life decisions, like signing on to a bachelor degree course that will cost you thousands.

Mostly, parents feel that they need to make decisions for their children because they are not capable of doing it themselves. You can build your parents' faith and trust by showing them you are mature enough to handle your own decisions and positively plan your own future.

Also, try to be brave and allow your intuition to have a voice. After high school, I looked into psychology and counselling courses but was told by an unfortunate influence in my life at the time that it was a boring profession, listening to other people's problems all day long. I listened and allowed myself to be influenced away from my intuitive thinking because I didn't know any better. Now, ten years later, I am a counsellor and have the privilege of supporting others through their darkest times, and helping them to make positive changes in their life. Not boring at all!

Who must you appease?

- Consider the people in your life, such as family members, friends and others, who influence your decisions. Are you able to be yourself around them?
- Do you have to change your thoughts, feelings or behaviour to please others?
- When you assert your real self, how do these people react?
- Consider at least three ways that you can take back control of the way you present your personality to the world, your actions and your decisions for your future.

If you are past the point of listening to your parents but still find yourself easily influenced by other people, you need to identify the areas of frustration in your current life, the things you aren't *sure* about that give you clues about where your heart really lies. If you secretly think that everyone you work with is a wanker, you have to question your real desire to want to climb the ladder in that field. It may not just be a work thing. If you find yourself internally cringing or pasting on a fake smile when talking to particular friends or family members, then you have to question your interest within the relationship as well.

Being comfortable in your own skin means you can make level-headed judgements and you don't have to feel as if you are able to be pulled with the tide of whoever is around you and their expectations of the person you should be. When you begin to know who you are and what you want out of life, you start to build a foundation where it's no longer necessary to do as people expect of you. You are in control.

Accepting the person that you are makes interaction with other people so much easier because you aren't as afraid that you'll look like an idiot or be exposed for the fraud that your inner critic says you are. You are enough. You are interesting. You are special. People want to know you and not a clone of a non-existent 'ideal'. If the people that you associate with don't like it when you assert your real self, then they are not supportive of your personal growth.

Judgement calls...

Think of a few times in your life where you have been swayed by other people to do or act as they have wanted but went against your own intuition. What was the outcome and how did it make you feel? How would it have been different if you had made your own choice? What stopped you from making your own judgement?

Conversely, think of a few times in your life where you haven't acted as your parents, friends, boss or someone else has expected of you. Were your actions justified? Why? How did it make you feel to make your own choice in this situation?

You do you...

Other people's opinions of you are actually none of your business. This took me a while to get my head around but it makes being and accepting myself much simpler. You don't need to worry about the thoughts in other people's heads if you believe in yourself and the actions you are taking. You are on a level playing field, even if it doesn't feel like it. You don't have competition because there is no one else on the planet who has your thoughts, your experiences, your physical, mental and emotional characteristics, your skills, your strengths, your weaknesses, your passions.

As model and burlesque performer Dita Von Teese once said, "You can be the ripest, juiciest peach in the world but there is always going to be someone who doesn't like peaches." Someone else's negative feelings or behaviour towards you are actually rarely about you. Openly displaying yourself as who you are and being confident enough to intuitively follow your path is deeply confronting for people who don't have the guts to do the same. If you are going to be great (which you are), then you need to expect negativity and rise above it. Another quote I love is, "If you want to avoid criticism, do nothing, say nothing and be nothing," by Aristotle. Continue to be you, and do you, no matter what they say.

It has taken me a long time to really portray my real self to the world. Don't for one minute think that I'm telling you it's easy but I am telling you that it will change the way you see everything. Accept who you are – even the bad bits. It makes it easier to survive. An example of self-acceptance is my personal acceptance of the fact that I have issues with seeking approval from others. Maybe it is the middle child in me. Even while writing this book, I would slip into conversations with friends about how it was going, fishing for interest. I'm often seeking validation from others, and now that I recognise my behaviour, it becomes less of a needy action.

Maybe it takes a lifetime to truly not care what other people think. Perhaps you are much stronger than me and already do not care. I have reached the point when at least I can call myself out on my habits. Now I notice if I am letting my need for approval get in the way of how I feel about myself. I am in the driver's seat of my own self-acceptance and self-validation. I make my own choices and listen to my internal wisdom, trusting that it will let me know if I'm starting to relinquish control and slip into a needy mindset. Personal growth is a continual re-evaluation of actual reality versus your own perception of reality.

Of course, there is always a tough balance between discovering your own strength and allowing yourself to be helped by others who might have had more life experience. You can deal with others' opinions with the respect they deserve but ultimately it is your life, your choice and you should back yourself. If you make a mistake then there will be a valuable lesson in it. Just be prepared for all consequences, because as an adult they will be your responsibility.

Be honest with yourself and listen to that little voice inside you that says, "This feels right." It will not lead you astray.

Chapter Seven
Monday Blues

As you move through your new adult life, the hazy fog of unhappiness can descend over you and settle insidiously within your determined daily routine. I continued living – working, eating and partying – for many years with good intentions of living a productive and happy life, but always with my head firmly in the future. In order to connect with my soul and start living a life that felt good, I needed to become aware of my experiences from day to day, what was bringing me joy and what wasn't. Life naturally ebbs and flows through good times and not so good, but I was accepting boredom, anxiety and misery as a normal part of the everyday. I committed myself fully to a grim routine of work and study.

In order to invite positive change, commit to honestly admitting the habitual stuff keeping you stuck.

The hardest part of growing up and moving into functional adulthood is the resistance to accept that we, alone, have the power to create whatever life that we want. Although once you let this realisation in, it is also the best part. But when you are stuck within the confines of your own self-made drudgery, it is incredibly difficult to understand how to pull yourself out of it and into a life that you deem worth living. That same power to create a great life feels like a heavy weight of responsibility and it might just be easier to snuggle back under the covers, thanks very much.

If your childhood was anything like mine, you had a certain amount of freedom and independence, in terms of being able to think your own thoughts and discover your own likes and dislikes, but when it came to dealing with anything with so much as a whiff of real adult responsibility, you knew it wasn't really up to you to be the decision-maker. So for the first time in your life, you become aware that the decisions are all yours. This could include things like what you eat for breakfast, whether you are going to show up for uni class today or if you are going to bother to lodge your tax return.

At first, making these choices without consulting anyone is exhilarating. "Yes," you say. "I would like McDonald's for breakfast, lunch and dinner. Yes, I will take a sickie from work to hang out with my boyfriend. Don't mind if I do." But once the reality of this sets in, the sudden weight of responsibility has a huge impact on your state of mind. Life becomes all about what we *should* be doing.

I'm not sure when it starts, but it might be a hangover from when we live with our parents and they either tell us, or there's a general unspoken understanding of, what we should and shouldn't be doing. Then we move in with roommates or friends who, unlike our parents, don't tower over our beds telling us to get up in the morning.

<u>Reflections...</u>

- In what ways did your parents act as the decision-makers throughout childhood?
- What level of control did you have on your own thoughts, actions and behaviour?
- How did this influence you as you left school and moved into the next stage of your life? List some positive and negative impacts.

Left to our own devices...

Without any parental influence, suddenly we are left to our own devices, which feels great for a while. You would think we would just go ahead and continue down the path of endless freedom and joy. But instead, we feel the weight of big decisions ahead. We want to be independent and adult but get a bit nervous at the prospect of being left to our own devices for the first time. We begin to engage with the little voice of judgement inside us, which grows continually louder to keep our actions in check, just like our parents used to.

Sometimes our internal dialogue has good intentions. After all, most of us are intending to become a fully-fledged, respected member of society, with a job, perhaps a qualification of some sort, certainly a plump bank balance and maybe even a life purpose if we're lucky. We drag ourselves out of bed to a job or study that we hate because we *should*. Regardless of how bad our Monday Blues get, we don't quit. We accept that Mondays suck, along with the rest of the days of the working week and we keep pushing, trying to do something and be somebody.

Other times it's not as helpful. For instance: "I should be skinnier." "I should have a better face." Or, "I should be more popular." In times of weakness, the dialogue gets even more creatively self-deprecating: "I should have more money." "I should have better clothes." "Someone should be in love with me." Or, "I should be more established in my life by now." There are a million versions of the same phrase and depending on the issues most relevant to you, you will be aware of that manic Tinkerbell who lives on your shoulder and whispers to you that you aren't very interesting and nobody really likes you.

There's really nothing good about being caught up in your own head this way. These negative thinking patterns create other psychological and emotional situations for ourselves. Constantly putting yourself down, on top of the general confusion and pressure of growing up and learning who you are, causes unnecessary stress and insecurity. This feeling is usually supplemented by the continual comparison of your life to others' lives especially through the easily accessible and ever-available social media channels, resulting in jealousy and the aching loneliness that accompanies it.

Personal reflections...

- What are some of the judgements you make or *shoulds* that you tell yourself? Which ones are helpful (e.g. I *should* go to uni today) and which ones are harmful (e.g. I *should* have a flat stomach)?
- How do the helpful *shoulds* keep you in line to achieve tasks?
- How do the harmful *shoulds* contribute to the way you feel about yourself?

Sad face...

Physically there are other symptoms also. Do you get headaches? Tight neck and shoulders? Stomach cramps? Over-emotional after a big weekend? These may be manifestations of tension, over-thinking, holding the weight of the world on your shoulders, resistance to change and the anxiety caused by fear of moving forward. Stress has been scientifically proven to lower the function of our immune system, so if you are continually coming down with a flu or tonsillitis or just generally feel *crap,* it's time to look inward. This is especially the case if you are anything like I was at that time, lacking respect for the future so much that I mistreated my body with anything that would give me immediate gratification.

Living in Australia, we have such an ingrained drinking culture, that if you tell people you are staying sober at any given event, they look at you as if you've told them you've accepted a seat on Richard Branson's next flight to space. When I was growing up, my mum would fall asleep on the couch after dinner with a glass of wine in her hand and never spill a drop. It's a skill she still brags about. Having a drink is *just what you do* to decompress after a day's work, to celebrate any occasion or because it's after midday (unless of course it's Champagne and orange juice because, darling, that's just part of a balanced breakfast).

If you like Pina Coladas...

I was drinking at high school sleepovers and parties from the age of fourteen. As a girl, if you could somewhat handle your booze, you were more accepted into cooler circles and definitely deemed more worthy to hang with the guys. I would drink pretty much anything I could get my hands on – unusual spirits stolen from my parents' 'cooking' stash, cask wine or Passion Pop mixed with juice, Woodstock or UDL cans, or any other pre-mixed drink that the grey-haired chaps in charge now call Alcopops.

Once I moved out of home, the easy drink of choice would be a bottle of vodka with whatever sugary mixer would make it palatable. Earning my own money meant I could experiment with different variations of spirits with juice and soft drinks, and these were the glory days before spirits were so heavily taxed. When I was flat broke, my mum would gift me cheap bottles of red which I would drink on a quiet night in with the girls – it felt like a healthier option, like grape juice. Heaps of antioxidants.

I was definitely more confident on the piss and could just let loose and be myself. Quite a relief to have a laugh when the rest of my week felt so grim. My bonds of friendship felt tangibly stronger with every boozy girls' weekend. It was definitely easier to meet and talk to guys when I was pissed.

When I worked in corporate property, it was not uncommon to go to lunch with the other secretaries and have a wine or two, or for business meetings to be accompanied by a couple of beers at three p.m. until late.

When I was hungover though…woof. I couldn't look at myself in the mirror. I'd be cringing about whatever heinous thing I'd said, who I'd made out with and how many cigarettes I'd smoked. My fingers would be yellow and my face would look prune-ish. I was always terrified to look at my bank account. And I'd spend the rest of the week feeling sad, lonely, anxious and generally unwell, until I followed the cycle all over again the next week.

Of course, I don't regret a thing. Our younger years are supposed to be wild, with our vibrant energy and ability to back-up. Once you get past twenty-five, hangovers become almost unbearable so you must make the most of multiple nights out per weekend. And I did. No doubt you will too. I had every right to be a loose unit and so do you. I'm not saying this to make you feel any differently.

I only wish it might not have been so utterly necessary to escape from my real life. I only wish I might have been as brave when I was sober.

Without wanting to sound like a Government-funded Public Service Announcement, cringing every Monday about what happened on the weekend doesn't have to part of your norm even if it's everybody else's. When you create a life you aren't trying to run away from, it becomes less necessary to escape. Drinking becomes about having a good time, not a means to forget trauma. Connecting internally to the person that you are naturally creates better self-awareness and a more harmonious relationship between your life and your consumption.

Drinking with our friends and colleagues appeals to our sense of community and reinforces our relationships. It's ingrained into our culture and society's expectations. It's a great confidence booster, it dulls those pesky insecurities and it's your wingman when you're on the prowl. Plus, nobody wants to be the odd one out. Ever been the sober one when everyone else is drunk? Jokes are less funny, slurred conversations rattle on for hours and eventually it's an emotional bloodbath. Your friends perceive you as boring or a party-pooper, no matter how much you protest.

Drinking to get drunk is a bit of a self-perpetuating cycle, though. It feels great at first because it deadens any intense feelings you might be experiencing – boredom, sadness, loneliness, etc. But then the next day, they multiply tenfold and, if you're anything like me, you're an anxious and depressed wreck, no matter how good your night was. At such a sensitive time of life, when you finally have the opportunity to address some of the negative self-beliefs from childhood and adolescence, further drama can be damaging. The negative experiences that inevitably attach themselves to drinking too much become firmly imprinted on your raw adult psyche. And there they remain, until you're willing to go deep enough to deal with them.

Get amongst it. Be loose. Join in. But just remember that once the booze wears off, all you are left with is the memory (or worse, the blank hole in your memory) and the awful sinking feeling that you've embarrassed yourself again, fallen over drunk, flashed your boobs, posted an awkward status update, had sex with your ex, lost all of your belongings and told your friend what you really thought about her even though it was super hurtful, and you're not sure if everyone is going to hate you now or ever invite you to anything again. No harm in having a good time – unless there is.

If you are putting stuff (booze or anything else) in your body because you want to feel prettier, cooler, funnier and more interesting, just stop for a minute and think about it. How cool and pretty do you feel on a Sunday morning? If you are waking up with no regrets, like *really* no regrets, not just *denial,* no regrets, then go, you good thing. Conversely, if you feel sad, lonely and anxious, it's likely that your poor little soul is taking more of a battering with every sip, snort and four a.m. cheeseburger.

I know this because I spent years wearing those shoes. Even now, every once in a while, I try them on to see if they still fit. They do, but those fuckers still hurt my feet.

Personal reflections...

- How do you use escapism, either through alcohol, cigarettes, drugs, food or something else? Remember, this is not about taking away your right to have a good time, but more about self-awareness.
- Think of the way you feel after a big night–in what ways is it worth it, and in what ways is it not worth it?
- List some of the ways that being aware of these escape routes would improve your quality of life and your ability to deal with any deeper issues going on.

Bright, shiny objects...

It's much easier to find distractions from our inner voice, than to sit with the uncomfortable feeling of knowing things aren't great but not having any idea what to do about it. In this day and age, we have all the apps we could possibly want at our fingertips – messaging, social media, videos, streaming of shows and movies, games, online shopping and good old-fashioned email. No need to ever be truly alone again, we are connected to everyone at all times. I can literally spend half a day just jumping from one platform to another to see what's up, until my hand is tingling from holding my phone, my neck is sore from looking downwards and my battery is at a dangerous eleven per cent. My phone has been my biggest procrastination tool as a student and a writer.

Food can be another diversion from feeling anything too confrontational. Emotional hunger gets confused for real hunger and food becomes a way to fill ourselves up and attempt satisfaction, although it never lasts long enough. Soon that niggle returns and we head to the fridge or the shops down the road. I'm particularly familiar with being so chronically bored with my daily routine that I need to dream about my next meal or snack constantly to have any excitement or enjoyment whatsoever in my day. Lunch was always the highlight of my day when I was working full-time in a job I resented and I've always been an emotional eater.

If you are not treating yourself well, particularly with food and booze, you can be forgiven for not knowing better because you're young, you're learning, you've got that awesome metabolism and you bounce back pretty quickly. But at the end of the day, it comes down to whether you want to continue to keep allowing yourself to be carried from moment-to-moment stimulation and gratification to get you through each day, week or month, while your mind simultaneously ponders the past and panics about the future. Be real with yourself here. I think it might be that you want more, and you need more. Your actions are a choice.

Personal reflections…

- What distractions and avoidance techniques have you used in order to escape dealing with change? I personally used food as a distraction, the party lifestyle, and seeking out friends more troubled than I was to take the focus away from myself. Be honest and list as many distractions as you can.
- How did these distractions hold you back from moving forward?
- Do any of these distractions still play a role in your life now?

You are now experiencing the adult world with the growing desires of an adult and the developing body of an adult but with the social patterns of a teenager. And that's okay. This is not me telling you that you are young and silly. It's the opposite – you are strong, you are willing, you are growing. This is the rite of passage that you now must be subjected to for the purpose of learning. These are actual physiological changes that take time so that you can cultivate yourself into a more mature being with better perspective and understanding.

If things are feeling confusing, shameful, embarrassing and lonely, then understand that this is the way it is for much of your late-teens and early-twenties. The cavernous sensation of hopelessness that you're feeling inside, that hollow pit of being totally lost and confused, is completely normal. Acknowledging your thought and behaviour patterns is the first step towards making things easier, being kinder to yourself and ultimately moving past the victim mentality, putting you back in control.

Let's not beat around the bush – this is full-blown mental and emotional upheaval that you're dealing with, but learning when to get real with yourself can lighten the burden and stop you from stabbing yourself in the eye.

They don't teach you in school who you really are so you come out into the world searching for the section of the jigsaw that you might best fit. In fact, I'm not even sure that society encourages us to find ourselves at all, even as adults. I suppose we are more likely to become a cog in its wheel if we remain in the dark about who we are and what we want, instead spending our whole life in our nine-to-five job, drinking copious amounts of wine and buying assets on credit to fill our voids.

Also, part of learning about yourself is learning who you are *not*, so if you've spent a few years setting up a life that you now have discovered you hate, well done for identifying where you *don't* want to be. There is nothing wrong with starting over, whether it is physically in a new city, professionally in a new career, socially with a new circle of people, or emotionally with a new you.

It's a little vulnerable, yes, maybe a touch undignified to go against the grain of what you've always done. But when you consider the 'safer' alternative – remaining on a path of contempt for yourself and the blatant inadequacies in your life – it is preferable. Better to self-destruct now than to wake up one day as a lonely forty-year-old, never having done a damn thing for yourself and accepting a pitiful existence for so long that you're too scared to try anything new.

It can be dreadfully overwhelming to realise that you are solely responsible for your life now and nobody else. It might be a sad and even disappointing realisation, especially if you've come out of childhood expecting things to be as easy as they've always been. Or conversely, maybe you felt that with your new adult freedom, it would be like taking a break from the chains of being too young to change your circumstances. Like being in control would come naturally now that you've shed the weight of other people's control or expectations.

Either way, now that you're here, it can feel like you've been sailed out to the middle of the ocean and you've jumped in for a quick dip, but when you come up for air you realise the boat is gone. And fuck, what was that, that just bumped against your leg? You're stuck, drowning, treading water, drifting with the tide, waiting desperately to be spat back onto whatever beach will have you.

You don't have to accept this feeling of 'stuckness' in your own life forever. There may have been warning signs and reality checks that you've been ignoring. Perhaps you're within a personal crisis right now and you're not quite sure which direction to take. Maybe you're asking for advice from anyone who'll listen. Are you trying to avoid the truth from your own inner voice? If you keep looking externally for answers, what is your heart saying right now that you don't want to hear?

Personal Reflections

To get you back in touch with your intuition, let's reflect on some of the ways in which you distract and divert away from your personal truth.

- What current negative thinking pattern would you like to change? For instance, dwelling in the past, panicking about the future, avoiding your true feelings, thinking negative thoughts about yourself or other people.
- How would it improve your outlook on life if you were to change these thought patterns?
- What are the warning signs or the reality check that is popping up in your life, forcing you to start looking inward and listen to your heart?

Chapter Eight
All That Glitters

Success. Such a loaded word. For me, it conjures up mental images of rolling around in a bed of cash, private jets, expensive cars, flashy jewellery, spending holidays on a yacht and business meetings in fancy restaurants being served Champagne and canapés. Everyone loves a canapé. You're way more beautiful when you're successful too. Skinny, nice clothes, nails done – polished and effortless. Life is easy and you have all the time and resources to do whatever you want, whenever you want.

Success equals beauty, money, power and freedom.

Being successful means getting what you want. In order to truly know what you want, you first need to know who you are because having what you want is really just an extension of that. The goals that you then set in order to get what you want and therefore to achieve success must also encompass *why you want it*. Success is closely tied to our personal values, i.e. what is important to us (as discussed in Chapter Five).

When I moved out of home at eighteen, I desperately wanted success. To me it seemed like a mystical, faraway land where everyone was rich, happy and attractive (some days I look at my Instagram feed and still feel like that – and then I remember that even models have bad days, and real life differs greatly from a filtered snapshot). Back then, I wanted success but I also didn't feel as if I belonged in that league of worthy people. In fact, the kind of success that seemed realistic for me was rolling out of bed without a hangover and having a clean towel to use when I got out of the shower.

The divide between the normal level of functioning in day-to-day life and society's idea of success is huge. It's the Grand Canyon. We place celebrity culture and wealth on a pedestal. It creates this simultaneous desire to be a part of it and the fear that it's completely impossible to achieve, and that some miracle should need to occur between now and thirty for you to ever reach this dream. I used to secretly hope that a new talent I was previously unaware of would just miraculously emerge, bringing me fame and stardom, or that a wise, successful benefactor would take me under their wing and teach me the ways of success.

The reality is that success is super-achievable in our current world because of the opportunities available to us. Forget about society's definition of success and focus instead on understanding who you are, what you want and why you want it. Those are the factors that fill in the divide between your current life and a successful life. The essence of who you are will individualise the meaning of success for you and allow you to see it as a realistic goal, something that is meaningful to you and that is going to be a joy to work towards.

Images of Success...

- What images appear in your imagination when you think of success?
- Are these images part of society's definition of success or your individual definition of success?
- What kind of life do you dream of having? Imagine there are no limits.

Goal setting...

Most people shudder when the word 'goal' is mentioned, myself included. Setting goals feels like such a chore. So much easier to float through life and one day wake up with a million dollars on the beach in the Bahamas. The reason it feels like a chore is that we tend to formulate our goals and desires based on something that we think we want but are not sure how to get there, or the goal we set is not something we are actually excited about in our heart. This forces us to live our lives in grim determination to keep showing up for work, in order to make money so that one day we might be free.

The thing about success is we tend to frame it in our minds as a difficult to attain pipedream of mass fortune. At eighteen-ish years of age, we usually don't yet have a concept of what success really means and what it takes to get there. Even if our parents have been successful, we won't always relate to their version of success and it's normal to feel that almost everything our parents do is lame and boring. We want more than they have and we want it now. We are more up-to-date with technology and want more money for less hours at the office.

Success Reflections and Goal Setting...

Think about your current goals. Do they excite you? Make you scared? Bore you? Do they reflect what you want for your life, or a fabricated version based on what you were taught growing up?

Consider your goals in terms of the way you want to feel instead of what you hope to achieve or things you wish to attain. Write down five ways you want to improve the way you feel in the future. For example, you want to feel free, confident, satisfied, loved, etc.

Now rewrite your goals for your success in terms of short-term (actions/achievements for the next twelve months) and longer-term (actions/achievements for the next two years to five years). Dream big but also be realistic in terms of what you'll be able to achieve in that amount of time. Only include goals that align with your values and the way you want to feel in the future. Give each goal a 'why'. This will help you to emotionally connect to your goals and make them more realistic and achievable. For example, below is one of my current goals:

Short-term

Goal – *Start writing a second book*

Why? – *To continue to explore my creative interests and help others in their journey of personal development.*

Dreaming big...

In my first career path, I was set to become a hugely successful real estate agent, in my own mind. I'd had some sales administration experience and thought I was ready to plunge into a sales role. The agent I was assisting at the time went away on a six-week holiday, so I had my chance to prove myself. I could almost taste the commission that would be rolling in. Finally, this was my shot at the big league. I felt like Eminem in Eight Mile.

I really did do my best. But I discovered that I wasn't particularly good at small talk or getting to know clients and what they wanted. I found it difficult to relate to people who were old enough to actually own real estate or have the money to buy it. I cringed whenever anyone talked about how much money they had or assets they owned, which felt wanky and offensive. I had zero confidence in myself and my ability to sell anything at all. I realised just how long it would take and how hard I would have to work to live my initial dream. At that point, I focused my strengths on something I *was* good at – procrastinating at the office and pissing up my weekly pay after-hours.

What do you really want?

The thing is, if you define what success actually means to you and all the things you want from it, you can start to peel back the layers a bit and get to the core of what you really want. And then you won't need to wait, you can feel successful right now while you continue to grow and experience life. You can move ahead through life, learning about yourself, and updating your vision of success as you go. You are put back in control of your future and the way you feel about yourself.

Success to me was an end goal where I could finally have the freedom that I craved, the freedom to find myself, be myself and do what I wanted.

Success was never actually being a real estate agent. I just wanted what came after the money came – the freedom to travel, to live a lifestyle balanced between work and play, eat good food, be healthy and happy and beautiful. I wanted to be able to relax, maybe tap into my creative side, by having the space and the time and the energy to really explore and figure myself out. I wanted to be in a career that was meaningful, enjoyable and hopefully helped people in some way. I wanted to have nice things. I wanted to feel passionate and joyful and motivated.

Our personal meaning of success encompasses all of our inner connections to our deepest desires. It's craziness that we are still expected to participate in the rat race throughout our peak years, just so we might have enough to retire at sixty-five and THEN we can be free. Our parents' generation bought into this way of life, and who can blame them? They were just building on what they saw in their own parents' experience – a lack of jobs, food and other resources during the World Wars and the Great Depression. While there is nothing wrong with wanting to spend your life in one job making an honest living, the world has changed and brings with it the opportunity to live life the way you want to, without feeling bad about it.

Reflections for getting to the core of success…

Consider your personal values that you worked on in Chapter Five. How do your values reflect in your current career path? What is it about your career path or future plans that will reinforce your values and bring you joy, even when it's hard work?

Consider what your strengths and weaknesses are as a person. How might these factors play a part in your ability to reach your dreams? Do your strengths and weaknesses align with your current career path or plan of action? If not, how will you overcome this?

If you could wake up tomorrow and be successful and financially abundant, how would this change your life? How would you feel? What would you do?

Our relationship to money…

Growing up, my nickname from my parents was 'Top Shelf Laura', meaning that if I was allowed to choose something, like a present for my birthday or a restaurant to eat at, then I would always choose the best or most expensive option. It was drummed into me that choosing from the top shelf was not my place and that I should have been grateful even to have a choice at all. I'm sure that my parents were just mindful of creating spoiled brats for children, which I appreciate, but I'm fully aware now of just how easily negative connotations of money and success can survive our upbringing.

The capacity to make money and the ability to keep it in order to invest it wisely definitely requires a certain mindset and a positive relationship with having wealth. You often read about people winning the lottery and then being bankrupt within a year. Ignoring the core of what you really want, including your deepest emotional needs and your soul's purpose, will result in filling your life with things instead of meaning. There will always be more things to buy and you will never, ever fill an internal void of desire with possessions. You will still essentially have nothing.

Similarly, if you are constantly focusing on what you don't have, then you will be stressed and anxious about never having enough. With growing up comes certain responsibilities and it is challenging to see your hard-earned money flow out of your bank account for frustrating expenses like rent, car repayments and insurance. It's easy to get caught up in thinking about everything you have to pay, all the time. But when you live in the pattern of thinking that money is always going out and never coming in, no amount of money coming in is enough. Attracting more money into your life and forming good spending habits requires you to let go of negative beliefs about money, the attitude of lack, and the belief that it's bad to desire nice things.

There are lots of books specifically outlining steps to improve your own relationship with money and spending. Many of them focus on building value within your life through defining what is important, and appreciation for what you already have – a roof over your head, nourishing food and the things that we take for granted in our lives that don't have a price tag. An attitude of gratitude goes a long way to improving your outlook on money and life in general.

If you're anything like me, you're probably thinking that it's a lot easier to be grateful for what you have when you have a lot and near impossible to feel good about the emotional rollercoaster of barely scraping by from week to week. When you are in that zone, I completely understand how easy it is to get down and frustrated when you're watching all of your friends travel, have nice things and have no trouble affording going out all the time.

I have been there – as a student in my mid to late-twenties, I was studying well past the years that my friends were studying. They had begun their careers while I was working as much as I could at around fifteen hours a week and living out of home. Sometimes I would have to pretend that I was busy instead of telling them I couldn't afford to go out for drinks or dinner. You get sick of being *that guy* who is always complaining about money.

If you think of money as a symbol for other forms of freedom, stripping back the layers of your desire for more money will begin to identify what it is that you really want. Identifying why we want or *need* these things is important to get to the root of what's really going on. It may not immediately fill your bank account but it will change your perception of being broke and eventually will create a better relationship with having money. It will also feel much better to be improving the other factors in your life that are important to you, rather than just making money the scapegoat for everything wrong in your world.

For example, it's like saying, "I need a new dress," when really you're thinking, "I feel ugly and want to feel better about myself," or, "I need a coffee and a muffin," because you're really feeling, "I'm so bored at work that I'm falling asleep at my keyboard." You might be desiring a nicer car because you actually want people to take you more seriously, or thinking, "I need to buy lunch again today," because you were feeling lazy last night and couldn't be bothered getting prepared. Jealousy and envy about people having nice things or going out all of the time are usually rooted in our deepest self-esteem issues like, "I'm not special." "I'm not loved," or, "I'm not enough."

Money Reflections...

Think about the way your parents handled money/wealth when you were growing up. What kind of beliefs about money have you taken on board? Are they healthy or would it help you to rethink your relationship with money?

Consider the ways you believe that not having money is stopping you from doing or having what you want. Try to peel back the layers of each and see what lies beneath. For example, "Having no money means I can't buy new clothes." Is it about the clothes or the way you see yourself? Or, "Having no money means I can't travel." What is it about travel that excites you? Are you running away from reality?

Next time you are feeling bad about money or not having all of the things, peel back the layers and discover what is really there. You may not be able to use magic to change your bank balance but it will put you back in control of what you can change – your choices in career, relationships and life. Also, if you have trouble with being patient, like I do, remember that life is fluid and seasons do change. What your reality is right now may change very quickly, with a pay rise or finishing study to go onto full-time work.

Create a life you truly love...

It's easy to forget that success is relative to your stage of development. I do believe that it's great to dream big and that it serves no one to think small. Having said that, appreciate the journey every step of the way. You don't have to be earning hundreds of thousands of dollars each year and travelling the world to be successful, returning every couple of weeks to your massive inner-city home, hot life partner and angelic children. The reality of that kind of lifestyle brings with it its own challenges and pitfalls which tend to be forgotten or ignored when you're looking at it from the outside and wishing it was you. There is no skipping the hard part. That is why you need to find what you love and do that, so that the hard part doesn't cause a nervous breakdown.

Doing what you love is so important if you want to have a meaningful life and enjoy the journey to success. We see those catchphrases everywhere: 'Do what you love and you'll never work a day in your life' and so on and so forth. Well, it's not always that simple for everyone to discover their passion without having much experience in the real world to discover what is out there and what is possible. As an eighteen-year-old, I had no idea what I needed to do to match my current reality with the way I hoped I might one day feel and live.

The trick is not to get paralysed by overthinking every detail of your future but being honest with yourself and where your heart is leading you, understanding your strengths and weaknesses as a person, and experimenting with a flexible attitude. Go with the flow. Accept that it may take a minute to get yourself together onto a career path that you are passionate about.

Focus on developing a positive relationship with yourself and your abilities, a strong work ethic and a broad range of skill – nothing you learn is a waste. Be patient and you will eventually be grateful for every experience.

Once you begin to connect with yourself and start to discover what you love, you may hold the expectation that you'll slide right into instant success and automatically be the best. Because you love it and that's enough…I hate to burst your bubble but unfortunately it will still be a hard slog if you want to be successful. You will still suffer from dreaded procrastination and have days where you feel unmotivated. But the ups will be more significant than the downs. You will be able to look at yourself in the mirror each day and know in your heart that it is what you want at any stage of the journey, not just when the money comes. Trust your instinct and keep hustling.

Author Mark Manson wrote about the concept of a shit sandwich in one of his epic blogs about life purpose. He said that every dream comes with a shit sandwich, and that you will be forced to eat a shit sandwich no matter what you do in life, so you may as well do what you love. Eat the shit sandwich that comes with your truest passion. Finding your passion and knowing that you are willing to do it, every day, regardless of the shit sandwich you will have to swallow – *that is success*.

Success now...

When you think of success, do you become impatient? In what ways do you compromise what you truly want to obtain success or money sooner? How does this affect the way you feel about yourself in daily life?

Consider your current career path. Are you willing to continue to eat the shit sandwich in order to climb the ladder of success in this field?

Success is a reflection of your belief in yourself...

Finding and following your passion is the first step but becoming successful in your life and career requires a level of self-assuredness, something I was entirely lacking in the first ten years after high school. Well into my professional career and during my years as a student, I learned the hard lesson that if I didn't start believing in myself, no one else would. Believing in yourself is a process of accepting who you are, understanding your skills, having faith in your personal strengths, acknowledging your weaknesses, and uncovering the internal negative self-talk and self-sabotage patterns in all areas of your life.

Once you understand and accept all of these factors for yourself, it is easier to become comfortable with portraying yourself to the world in the way that you want to be seen. When you begin to align your authentic self with the way you want the world to see you, it builds self-confidence and clarifies your image. Essentially, this is marketing and this is how you create momentum towards a successful life.

This little piggy went to market...

In my early professional career, I had absolutely no confidence. When people asked me what I did for work, I would say I was 'just a secretary'. When I started studying, I was 'just a student'. I blushed if people asked me in-depth questions, thinking that I would make a fool of myself in front of someone who probably knew more about life than me and they would see straight through any thin veil of 'expertise' that I was pretending to possess.

When I started my counselling practice, I had to quickly become accustomed to marketing myself. For the first time, I was doing something that I really enjoyed and felt aligned with, which made it all the more challenging, knowing that such a large piece of myself was invested in this business. I had to understand what areas of counselling I specialised in and specifically how I could help my clients. I had to put all of that information into an attractive and clear package in order for people to choose my services over others. It still brings up mountains of self-doubt on my behalf – why should anyone think that I am the best? I'm sure there are others out there with more extensive experience, training and qualifications.

But I believe that this crucial component is why many people fail to make it in business – they do not know how to communicate what they do and why they do it, even to themselves because of the internal fear that they are not good enough or don't deserve success. Learning to put yourself out there and market yourself to others is a discovery process of self-worth and confidence. Marketing means being clear on who you are and what you do, and having the strength to put that out there to the public.

Even if you are working in a position where there is no self-promotion involved, you would still have a personal Facebook page, Instagram, Linkedin and other social media accounts. You would still be required to attend interviews for new employment positions, or meetings with external associates, or talk to strangers in some capacity about what it is that you do. This too is a form of marketing yourself to the world. How do you want people to see you? Professionally, being able to communicate effectively who you are and what you do unquestionably promotes your confidence and commands respect from others.

Self-promotion Reflections...

- How do you promote yourself and what you do to others? In what ways could you become clearer about your role, and how you communicate it to the world?
- Do you feel embarrassed when talking about what you do, and if so, why?
- How could marketing yourself to the world contribute to a stronger self-image and confidence?

Clear as mud...

Even if your future is unclear, getting clear on what you want will pave the path that otherwise remains unrecognisable. You must understand the difference between your version of success and what success means to the people closest to you – family, friends, boyfriend/girlfriend, etc. If your values are different, you run the risk of restricting your potential to fit in with their upper limit. If you know you are driven to achieve more than the people around you, you owe it to yourself to explore how far your own boundaries go rather than base the expectation of your life upon someone else's. Don't play small if your heart is asking you to dream big.

Choosing to keep supportive people around you will help you to see yourself and your work through their eyes. This can be validating to your gifts and purpose. Although, be careful whose opinion and support you seek – friends or family can sometimes be wolves in sheep's clothing. They will advise based on their own understanding of the world and fear of failure, which may not match up with your vision and will feel like a personal attack on your abilities.

Getting feedback from others was, and is, the hardest part of seeking guidance for me. If someone didn't approve of something I was doing, or I even caught a whiff of disdain or questioning, I would fall into an emotional heap. I still sometimes do, especially if I'm PMS-ing. I had to learn to trust my heart and continue down my path with courage. It's lonely sometimes. Not everyone understands what I do or why I do it. But for the first time, I don't feel like a fraud.

When you feel resilient enough, invite and welcome constructive criticism from people that you trust and respect, like a manager or mentor who is inspiring you and driving you to continue down your particular path. After some years of being disillusioned enough to think I had all of the answers for myself, I now try to listen more than I speak in an attempt to gain insight into better ways to do things. And if I'm given advice that doesn't sit well with me, I am strong enough and in tune with my intuitive purpose that I take what I need and let the rest go.

You are brave, even if you don't realise it...

Remove the burden from your shoulders that says you should have more things or be more established in your life. Identify your fears of failure. Go further and identify your fears of success. Accept, acknowledge and move past these fears so that you can bravely take your life to the next level.

And lighten up, for fuck's sake. I let my fears dictate everything I did or didn't do until I realised that this was a toxic way to live. Life doesn't have to feel like impending doom. It can be fun. If you don't make the conscious decision to enjoy the journey at every step, then you will be miserable because the roadblocks are inevitable. The more you try, the richer you will be in experience and your sense of self.

Life is just an experiment – have fun with it.

You are enough right now. If you build on that, great. If things fuck up, oh well. Expect that, at some point, you will likely experience frustration, lack, doubt and wanting to give up. And that's okay.

Because you won't give up. No matter what path you choose, you'll be great.

Action Steps for Career

- Look for role models who are living the life you dream of–but not just the Instagram kind.
- Develop your sense of purpose–think about your current job and brainstorm the purpose of your role. Do you connect with your purpose? Does it inspire you?
- Think about your dream job and the deeper purpose of it; for example, being a voice for people who are disadvantaged, challenging societal conditioning, creating sustainable methods to improve the environment, or helping people connect to their true potential.
- List all of the things you love and things you hate about your current job. Are you willing to eat the shit sandwich of your current job? If not, can you outsource that aspect of your job? Can you change/modify your role at work? Can you start your own business? Can you change your attitude?

Chapter Nine
I Am Woman

When I was in high school, I was addicted to *Dolly*, *Girlfriend*, *Cosmopolitan* and *Cleo*, and any other magazine that would help me to learn how to become 'a woman'. The articles were cheesy enough that even back then I cringed and giggled but I kept reading, hoping I would pick up key advice. *Dolly Doctor* confirmed that sleeping on my stomach would not make my boobs flatter. *Cosmopolitan* and *Cleo* guided me in all the tricks that would keep my man faithful and sexually satisfied, within the pages of their 'sealed section'.

As time passed I progressed to *Vogue*, *Marie Clare*, *Famous* and *OK!* I took in what every celeb was wearing and what diet they were following. I devoured all of it, unconsciously searching for the 'hack' to become beautiful, desired and empowered. I wanted to be a woman who was in control of how I looked, who I dated and who I had sex with. I wanted to feel good about my choices and my body. Let's be honest, I wanted boys to desire me. However, instead of making things easier and clearer, reading magazines deepened the pool of the unknown, the concept of sex and longing, and how that related to me as a girl growing into a woman.

My mum introduced the basics of sex and having babies to me when I was about six years old. She gave me this book to read called *Every Woman* and I was fascinated with the pages containing black and white sketches of the baby coming out of the vagina. I was so fascinated, in fact, that I took the book to school to show my friends and ended up getting in trouble because *Every Woman* also contained some fairly graphic illustrations of sexual intercourse.

My Grade One teacher (a twenty-something single mother) and the teacher in the classroom next door (a gay man) caught us giggling in confusion and amazement about such a baffling procedure of bringing life into the world. You would have thought these two may have been more open-minded given their own personal situations, but they were horrified that I could poison my friends' minds with such filth, and my mother was called.

I think I have always been a truth-seeker, partly because I'm intuitively aware of forces in the world that are bigger than me as an individual, and partly because I don't like to admit when I don't *get* something. Somewhat of an observer, I was always perceptive to conversations around me, looking for answers to the many private questions milling around my mind. Fast forward many painfully awkward years of searching through magazines and I finally realise that the secrets to understanding myself as a woman weren't within any of those pages.

Connecting to myself as a woman and feeling comfortable in who I was, was really about taking the time to discover myself and making a conscious decision to accept whatever I found. I already have the female anatomy and I emotionally identify with the female gender. I am a woman. There is no 'how to' needed to become what you already are. And there is no secret that everybody else knows and you don't.

The messages to keep our girlishness in check start from a young age. I remember my Grade Two teacher telling me to stop being so bossy when I was playing handball with the boys and that I should play by their rules, never mind that they were cheating. My best friend turned up to my seventh birthday party in hysterical tears because her mum had forced her to wear a dress. Subtle, seemingly harmless reminders that girls should smile, look pretty and remain quiet.

As we grow up, it just keeps coming – labels like 'frigid', 'slut', 'bitch', 'whore' and 'cunt' do the rounds. Popularity is based on appearance instead of kindness. My Year Ten homeroom teacher (male) told me that teaching at an all-girls' school was a bottom-rung position and he was hoping to be shifted into an equivalent job at an all-male school as soon as he could. That was right after he told me that I would be perceived as 'loose' by my friends and other teachers because he had seen me holding my boyfriend's hand that morning as we walked from the bus to our neighbouring schools.

None of these experiences broke me to a point where I couldn't survive. But it is interesting to think back and wonder how much the constant reference to my gender and the stereotype I should fit into shaped my self-esteem and my life choices. Building self-awareness into these subtle messages is another step towards breaking down unhelpful beliefs and negative self-talk.

Reflections...

Identify some of your own experiences with navigating being a girl, and growing into a woman. How might these experiences have shaped your own ideas about yourself, and beliefs about your place in the world?

I am woman...

I really do appreciate my 'woman-ness'. I am a communicator that loves to talk deeply about my thoughts, my feelings and my ponderings of the universe, and that might be harder to express as a man in today's world. I love the laughter, the joy and the energy that flows when a group of women get together to connect with and support each other. Femininity, to me, encompasses qualities that are soft and nurturing like patience, care, affection, intuition and sensuality. But I also think myself to be independent, disciplined, strong, focused, confident and free, which are typically 'masculine' traits.

Character Reflections...

- Consider your own personality traits. Do you consider yourself more typically 'feminine' or 'masculine'?
- As discussed in previous chapters, how well do you know, accept and love yourself? How has your strength of character improved by embarking on the journey of getting to know yourself?

Physical anatomy and gender don't define who we are as people. We need to discover the balance of so-called feminine and masculine qualities that make up our own individual and unique personality. Self-awareness is the key, not forcing yourself to fit into a gender stereotype. Our value as people, our strength and our frailty, our abilities and weaknesses, our character and integrity, are simply not linked with sex or gender. Being a strong woman does not necessarily require comparison to men, or even to other women. It comes back to being a strong person, and being a strong person means knowing, accepting and loving yourself.

Fitting a square peg in a round hole...

None of us are strangers to gender stereotypes, and these are largely a result of a historically patriarchal society and perpetuated by what we are fed by the media. As time progresses, ideas around gender and equality are expanding and becoming more fluid. There is more of a focus on humanity, and individuals are more able to thrive in their complexity and be whoever they choose to be. Women are encouraged to be strong, independent thinkers and men are invited to express their sensitivity and emotions.

The world we live in tends to favour personality traits that are assertive and motivated – people who get shit done. We revere business and productivity. For this reason, women with stronger 'feminine' qualities may find it harder to find their place. Becoming more in tune with your own personality means allowing yourself to become grounded in who you are. Prioritising your softness will need to be a more conscious effort and tactic of self-preservation in order to balance your authentic self with the behaviour that is encouraged by society.

They don't teach you in school how to allow your best qualities to come through naturally, and how it is possible to learn other traits that might not be typically what you would expect from a woman or a man. We must inspire these qualities in ourselves. To discover who we really are, we must give ourselves permission to tune into our depth as a human being, and express whatever feminine or masculine qualities we feel most connected to in that moment. This is an ongoing self-awareness and acceptance process.

Moving from Girl to Empowered Woman…

What are your own beliefs about men and women? Have you formed your own stereotypes about the abilities/strengths/qualities that women or men possess or do better than each other?

Consider your friendship group. Are they a group of empowered, strong women? In what way do you lift each other up? In what ways do you tear each other down? Do you have a lot of male friends? Do they have typically 'masculine' qualities? Do you change around your male friends, e.g. become more 'masculine'?

All the honeys, who makin' money...

Although gender equality is far from perfected, most women in the developed world are living the lives that the feminists of yesteryear fought for. Feminism goes so much deeper than bra-burning and Girls Can Do Anything posters, but sadly has almost become a dirty word. Terms like 'Femi-Nazi' do the rounds whenever a woman stands up for herself or poses a strong opinion, especially by keyboard warriors on social media platforms.

It makes me cringe every time I hear a prominent woman, or any woman for that matter, denounce feminism as if it's *embarrassing* and *unnecessary* instead of simply communicating the rights and needs of half the planet's population. The history of equality for women is complex, and to me, saying that feminism is just man-hating is like spitting in the face of women who grew up in a patriarchal world with no opportunities or rights.

Most women want to pursue careers and weren't raised to simply find a man who would support them. Women have passion, ideas and abilities. Even a woman who *chooses* to spend her life making babies and keeping a clean, well-stocked home for her equally hardworking husband (which is a perfectly respectable day-job, by the way) should want other women to have that same ability to choose to do what makes them happy. If we are all striving to live our best life then there is no reason to hold anyone else back from theirs.

True feminism is love and support for women in the interests of equal rights. It was born from women who believed in egalitarianism – equal rights for everybody regardless of gender. Feminist ideologies shouldn't create fear or division between genders but combine our strength for a better world.

Years ago, women across the world stood up to mainstream society to defend their honour, integrity and many of the basic rights we currently take for granted. We would live in a completely different society if these same women had simply sat back, paralysed by embarrassment, resentment and shame for wanting something more. We would live in a world where a female prime minister or president would simply not be possible.

It is our responsibility to understand the past struggles of women and the transformation of culture over the last hundred years (not a particularly long time when you think about it). These are our roots. Through the eyes of these women, we are reminded of our own strength, resilience and power to overcome. To respect their hard work means to respect this part of history and we can learn about the societal changes that we owe to them.

These women didn't hate men. But they did love themselves enough to speak up.

A history lesson in a nutshell...

First Wave of Feminism – late 1880s to early 1900s:

- Focus on suffrage (a woman's right to vote and participate in Parliament), and the right to own private property;
- Back then, women rarely worked, unless they were factory workers, seamstresses, wet nurses (mobile breast-feeders), occasionally teachers, and prostitutes (the oldest profession in the world), and therefore had little capacity to determine their own financial future. They were instead expected to be mothers and control the home like a domestic goddess;
- Opportunities for women increased in the early to mid-1900s, because many men went to serve in the First and Second World Wars, and women began to prove their legitimacy in a range of professions, although they were paid around a third of the wage.

Second Wave of Feminism – mid-1900s until the 1980s:

- Achieved huge progress in sexual freedom and reproductive rights for women;
- Women were beginning to be seen as separate sexual entities from men with their own desires and plans for the future, and were able to gain control over their own bodies and subsequent sexual choices;
- Feminists rallied for safe and legal abortions. In 1973, the landmark Roe vs. Wade case in the U.S.A. legalised abortion for the first and second trimester (in some Australian states, abortion is still regarded as a criminal offence);
- In Australia, the 1980s brought the decision that it was unlawful in all states of Australia for a man to sexually assault his wife. Until then, a woman was legally a man's property upon marriage.

Third Wave of Feminism – 1980s to present time:

- Focus on contemporary issues including(but not limited to) an individual's freedom to express their sexuality, campaigns like Free the Nipple exploring women's rights to show their body without being objectified body positivity movements, the culture concerning, slut-shaming and victim-blaming, gender fluidity, domestic violence, sexual discrimination and the gender pay gap.

The women who stood up for our rights weren't different from you and me. They probably didn't have a five-year plan in which they would casually change society. They, too, were normal twenty or thirty or forty-something-year-old women with plenty of fear for the future, but just a little bit more hope. They weren't sure if the world would agree that they had something important to say. Even so, they identified that something was fundamentally wrong and they stood up and said their piece anyway.

Current gender-based issues are continuously splashed all over the media, which simultaneously brings needed attention to them, as well as desensitising us. We have more forms of communicating these issues and commenting on them than ever before, through social media and other online platforms. Women are making history and this is being publicised more than ever. Julia Gillard's speech on misogyny in Parliament was a ground-breaking moment in Australian politics. Role models like Malala Yousafzai are celebrated for humanitarian work.

Products of Hollywood...

Of course, there are still many famous women who are just really, really ridiculously good-looking – shallow ideals based on appearance will probably always exist. But now more than ever we are celebrating strong and funny women who push the boundaries to shift the chauvinism, whether they are activists, actors, comedians, authors, musicians or sports stars. Terms like 'plus size' are being challenged and the portrayal of an ideal body type is starting to shift.

Have you heard of the Bechdel Test? It was formulated by Alison Bechdel in the 1980s to call out sexism in movies. The three main components of the Bechdel Test that allow a movie to be judged in terms of role equality are:

- Are there two or more women in the film, and do they have names?
- Do the women talk to each other?
- Do they talk to each other about something other than a man?

The movie must tick off all three to pass the Bechdel Test. You would think that it would be easy but some of the most famous movies of all time don't come close. You can Google all of the successful and popular movies that fail miserably – there's multiple websites of lists. Have a think about your favourite movies and think about whether they pass the test.

It's important to note, of course, that a movie which does pass the Bechdel test is not necessarily equal in gender representation, nor does it automatically express views or issues that are important to women. The Bechdel Test was designed to be tongue-in-cheek, so it isn't a failsafe but it's an interesting place to start in order to get your head around the subtle messages that are continually imprinted on our subconscious minds by media sources. It is worth becoming as educated as possible on the indirect ways that our world views are moulded by society, media and the entertainment industry.

Actresses are now using their platforms on social media and during award acceptance speeches to call out the misogyny and gender pay gap within the entertainment industry. Although, when it comes to equal pay, there is still a way to go across the board of almost all industries in the labour market. In almost all fair studies, that compare wages between men and women in a range of industries and roles, women still only earn between eighty to ninety cents where a man has earned a dollar for the same job.

Feminism Reflections...

- Do you identify with being a feminist? Why/why not?
- Are you compassionate towards other women? What are your thoughts on body-shaming, slut-shaming and victim-blaming?
- In what ways can you extend compassion and empathy to other women in daily life?

Authentically you in an inauthentic world…

These are interesting times and our world seems to be continually changing at an increasingly rapid rate. Mostly this is healthy conversation leading to positive progression on many traditional views. We are exposed to more information than ever before. For this reason, there are more opinions thrown about than ever before, and certainly social media and online forums play a huge role in this.

And yet, there is still pressure. Insidious pressure that creeps into our lives without much fanfare. The pressure for us to be smooth, hairless creatures of a certain size and shape. The pressure to put out. The pressure to be effortlessly attractive. The new type of Instagram pressure to be always living life to the fullest, to be 'authentically you', to be blessed. When did it become so important to have a beautiful-looking life? How many selfies does it take to capture the most 'authentic' angle? Isn't it more rewarding to have a life that feels good from the inside? These destructive messages bombard us at the most sensitive of times, when we are shaping our self-image and understanding of who we are.

Everyone experiences pressure – male, female, non-binary – we all do. However, there are just some issues that women face that are exclusive to having a vagina. Like, making a decision about when to leave (or pause) a career to have a baby, or the decision to terminate an unplanned pregnancy. The tax on tampons because they're a 'luxury item', FFS. Assumptions that you're cranky because you have your period. Having a terribly painful or heavy period or depressive PMS symptoms and having to push through it in secrecy because it's a woman's issue and not a real illness.

True blood...

The menstrual cycle is a funny thing. When you're a teenager awaiting its arrival, you look forward to it because it's like being in an exclusive women's club where the only initiation is bleeding once a month. Once you get it, you hate it because you bleed once a month. It's a hassle, it can hurt and it makes you feel crappy and cranky. You crave sugar and carbs and feel like a whale for four to seven days. Getting accustomed to the whole process of bleeding is pretty gross, and everyone's experience of having their period is different so it can be awkward to talk about for fear that yours is weird or wrong.

My parents separated when I was nine, so from that point I spent every second weekend at my dad's place. One fateful weekend at fourteen years old, I woke up to some unusual blotches on my boxer shorts. I had to have the cringe-worthy conversation with my dad that I had got my first period. He sourced me some football-sized pads and I stayed in bed most of the weekend, partly excited that I was a woman, and partly humiliated and sorry for myself.

These days I am not embarrassed that I get my period. Half the planet has, or has had/will have, a menstrual cycle, unless they are on some contraceptive that blocks it, or are pregnant, or are hormonally challenged. That doesn't mean that I have to shout it from the rooftops or that I don't ever get stung by the inconvenience of the whole thing, but I have consciously let go of the feelings of shame, frustration, discomfort and indignity I once felt. It's an opportunity to privately check in with my body, my mind and my spirit.

I now mindfully take the chance once a month to care for myself. Whilst life inevitably goes on during this time, I try to be more conscious of listening to my body and taking note of my physical, mental and emotional symptoms. I move a little slower and rest a little more. I cry if I need to cry (usually at an ad on TV or because my cat did something adorable). I try to hold my tongue if I want to explode about something that's angered me and wait to see if it's still an issue in three days' time. I buy myself some dark chocolate, make myself a Chai and let myself wallow in my emotions a little bit. Then a few days later, I emerge from the experience relatively refreshed and I continue on with business as usual.

I spent so many years resenting a biological fact, blocking it with the Pill and making up excuses to tell guys why I can't have sex so that I don't have to confront them with the uncomfortable truth that I was shedding the lining of my uterus. I've made a conscious decision that I no longer have time for that. I appreciate that my period gives me an excuse for time out. There's a silver lining for every inconvenient experience we face in this world, and finding it is a choice that we can make.

How do you feel about your menstrual cycle?

It might feel like a crazy notion to accept and forgive your menstrual cycle for the pain, inconvenience and mess. But it's here to stay, so you can spend your life fighting it or use it to enrich your connection with your body. Check in with your attitude towards your cycle with these questions:

- Do you purposely stop yourself from getting it each month with contraception?
- Can you talk about it easily with your friends and your partner?
- When you do get it, does it feel healthy?
- Other than being an inconvenience, what feelings come up when you know it's coming?
- Do you resent it or hate it or think it's gross? If so, why?
- Consider the silver lining of your own menstrual cycle. What benefits does it have?

The process of listening to my body means that I know it a lot better. Your menstrual cycle can give you valuable insight into your general health and hormonal wellbeing. I've learned how to track my cycle and like clockwork each month I know what's going on inside me. I even know what nutritional imbalances contribute to my painful and heavy periods, and which foods I should avoid to make my cycle almost symptom-free. It's a way for me to connect with myself. And because I'm not planning on pregnancy any time soon, each cycle brings a rushing sense of joy and relief that there's no bun in my oven.

I woke up like this...

Feminism doesn't mean having to become more like a man in order to be taken seriously and considered as equal. It is accepting femininity for what it is – a hot mess of passion, ability, strength, desire, thought and creation – and allowing that bubbling energy to evolve into an equally contributing source to society and the world.

I think it's not only possible but essential to embrace our 'woman-ness' and see that as feminism. Feminism equals freedom to follow what is in our hearts, to acknowledge our individual strengths and weaknesses, whatever that looks like.

Being a Confident Woman

There is a difference between having confidence and believing in yourself, and being egotistical and Narcissistic. The 'selfie society' we live in seems to embrace a culture of self-obsession. Although it's great to be confident and back yourself, it is also important to remain humble and good-natured at the same time. I've outlined the differences below:

- Narcissism features feelings of superiority, constant comparison to others, defensiveness, a need to be the centre of attention, being critical of others at the same time as being sensitive to others' opinions and judgement.
- Self-belief and confidence feature quiet pride in yourself and your work, humbleness, support for others in their chosen endeavours, a sense of purpose and mission in one's own path and the ability to self-congratulate and self-validate throughout the journey.

Yes, you are special. Yes, you are important. Yes, you are gifted–but equally so to every other soul on this planet.

You are who you are. A girl, a woman, a human being. Society may see you as 'feminine' or 'masculine' but you can make the choice to live outside of the box. You will adapt and change with the seasons of your life. Growing into your strength as a woman will come naturally as you discover who you are as a person. Let us no longer be shameful and resentful of our bodies, because they are not failing us by being 'uncomfortable' but they are serving us by giving us a vessel to reach our fullest potential. Let us be proud of who we are at every step of the journey, and continue to strive for our dreams, no matter how much they change along the way.

You've got this, girl.

Chapter Ten
She Bangs

Sex. Shagging, screwing, banging, fucking, bumping uglies, afternoon delight… However you like to refer to it, it is possibly the strongest of innate physiological drives for the animal species after hunger and thirst. Humans do it for fun, for intimacy, for pleasure and of course, reproduction. It's hard not to think about it once you learn about it and when you don't know much about it, it's like the giant elephant in the room encompassing both fear and desire. Your first few times may have felt like a bit of a let down – some mildly painful pumping resulting in a hot, wet mess. But somehow you've stayed curious.

I was inquisitive about sex from a fairly young age, which I think is quite a normal thing if you're honest with yourself. My childhood best friend and I used to take turns kissing Simon, one of the boys in our pre-school class, inside the cement tunnel in the playground. I have vague memories of exploring and comparing anatomy with other girls. Nothing sinister or scandalous, just shameless gathering of information.

Somewhere along the way throughout my childhood, sex became this big confusing thing that seemed largely clinical, mainly for mums and dads that were making babies. This was before the days of the internet so I only knew about what we learnt in Sex Ed from movies and television, and of course my favourite illustrated book, *Every Woman*. I understood that men and women lay in bed together and there was something more that happened between the sheets. I wasn't sure of the actual logistics, like what happened to your legs while this was going on. It seemed to me that they would be very much in the way.

My mum is very realistic and practical so she was great about communicating the bare facts and anatomical basics of sex and reproduction. However, I knew nothing about the natural human desire of sexuality. To be fair, my mother was one of eleven kids in a traditional Catholic family so I doubt sex was a topic discussed openly at family dinners. I considered myself lucky not to be one of those girls whose mother tried to be their best friend and initiated embarrassing conversations about the boys they liked and different sexual positions.

The awakening...

After learning the basics at a young age and then losing interest for some years, I began to get really curious about sex again at around eleven or twelve years old, about the same time that I started wearing a training bra and playing Spin the Bottle at birthday sleepovers. By then, I had some firmly lodged negative beliefs about how attractive I was and how capable I was at doing things, so it's no surprise that my feelings about sex were confusing, wrapped up in my own image of myself.

I wore glasses and braces, I was bad at sports and felt more comfortable with my head in a book than talking to real people (especially boys), so how was I ever going to be good at something with such serious implications? Sex was like the most advanced adult activity there was and it involved another person judging my appearance and abilities, and a whole array of foreign sensations. It felt like everyone knew more about it than I did, that it would come naturally to others but not to me. I was fascinated by it and yet unbearably awkward.

Awakening Reflections

- What age did you begin to be curious about sex? How did you begin to explore sexual feelings?
- Were your parents open with you about sex, and was that helpful for you?
- Are there past experiences or trauma that make you feel uncomfortable about sex? (These may be best explored with a counsellor or health professional.)

The first time, not the best time...

I lost my virginity at fifteen to a guy that I wouldn't even speak to, or maybe even recognise, if I passed him on the street today. He was my boyfriend for about four weeks until he stopped texting me back. I don't remember being particularly upset, though. He had served his purpose. He was a bit older and fairly attractive, even though he sometimes flirted with my friends in front of me. He wasn't a terrible person, just a typical teenage boy hedging his bets with all of the ladies. He treated me well, at least considering my awfully low standards at that age and I liked him because he liked me.

He was of partly Filipino descent and had a tiny penis but it didn't bother me to be honest. I had only seen a few and they all looked alien – I tried not to stare. We were in a spare room at his friend's house. I was on top and he tried to squeeze it inside my tight, uncharted territory. I didn't tell him it was my first time. He never asked. It was over really quickly and it never happened between us again. I was glad to be rid of the 'virgin' label and relieved I could move on with my life.

The second time I had sex, I knew the guy involved was a virgin and so I pretended I was too. I didn't want to look like a slut or be expected to perform considering I still had no idea what I was doing in the bedroom. It was about six months after my first time, I had not long turned sixteen. He communicated through his friends to my friends that he had a crush on me after meeting me at a 'gathering'. All of my friends thought he was divine. I was unconvinced but it felt good to be desired by someone who was so desired by everyone else.

My friend, who was dating his friend, organised drinks at her place on a weekend when her mum was away. It happened twice that night and, as if my body knew how to keep up with my virgin story, I even bled a little bit. I think it was because he was a bit too eager. We parted ways the next day, and I literally never heard from him again (even though we still have mutual friends). Yeah, he was a jerk actually. I was partly relieved but mostly offended, even though in my heart I felt no connection with him. I dated others guys but didn't have sex again for another year after that experience.

Keeping up with the Krowd...

Before I lost my virginity, I had a few other sexual encounters. Kissing boys at school dances and parties eventually progressed to other things. I sometimes felt the subtle pressure from a guy to do things that I didn't really want to do. I certainly felt the general pressure to keep up with the expectation that I would continue to develop sexually. A lot of that was my own expectation of myself to keep up with or surpass my friends' experience levels, even if it gave me a weighted feeling in the pit of my stomach. It was important to me that I fitted in. And naturally I had desires, urges. Teenage hormones were coursing through my blood. I wanted to feel wanted.

I hear stories about girls who encounter their first time with a boy that they loved and felt comfortable with. Part of me envies the tenderness of that kind of experience, like maybe I missed out because I was in such a rush to get it over with. But I wasn't emotionally mature enough to feel real love for someone in my teenage years, only infatuation. I didn't yet love or understand my own inner self, let alone have the capacity to be able to invite someone else into my private muddle of thoughts and feelings. Looking back, I don't have regrets about my resolute approach. That was my own process of learning.

Nonetheless, I look back on early sexual experiences and cringe. The first time I gave a blowjob was a while after I had lost my virginity. It was in the back seat of a car and I persevered with dogged determination for forty-five minutes, an absolute eternity. I didn't know if I was 'allowed' to stop before he came, so I just kept going, unsure of whether I was causing pleasure or injury. I eventually emerged triumphant with stiff limbs, a soggy dress, an aching jaw and an invitation to a school formal.

Despite my awkwardness and immaturity, I got on with it and forced myself into experiencing the uncomfortable world of sex. I looked at all forms of sex as cumbersome milestones, just getting it done so I didn't fall behind. I never liked to admit if I hadn't done something, or didn't understand first-hand what everyone else was talking about. Sex was consuming back then.

Sometimes I had fun and sometimes I didn't. Sometimes I felt empowered and sometimes I didn't. Sex certainly made things more complicated and heightened my already wild, teenage emotions.

At school lunch-time, my friends and I would swap stories about what had happened over the weekend, at school dances or parties or 'gatherings'. Pashing, fingering and wristies, giving and receiving head, and actual sex were dissected and discussed at length. If anyone had a banana on hand then there would be a re-enactment of technique. We would laugh and congratulate each other on a job well done, or commiserate if things had been awkward or turned out badly.

Occasionally I would feel a flicker of shame about how things were progressing. I don't know why that was but maybe the fear of moving towards an unknown destination, and the realisation that once the train had departed, there was no way back. Part of me craved the simpler times where boys and girls could be friends without the complication of sexual feelings. Coming from an all-girls' school, contact with the male species was limited and I was still getting used to being friends with boys.

Early days...

Even if you're not having sex for the first time, it's frigging awkward if you're new to it and not yet comfortable with your own anatomy and ability. You are literally stripped bare and exposed in all of your vulnerability. I always thought I should have these secret porn star abilities to impress the guy I was with. Conversely, it was all pretty stock-standard missionary position in the early days because I didn't know how to do anything else. Sex with someone you barely know is only partly fun and mostly awkward, and something will inevitably happen to make it more so.

When I was nineteen, I lived in the middle of the city and spent a lot of time drinking at clubs. I met a super-cute guy (or at least I thought so at four a.m.) who came back to my place for my first ever one-night-stand. We hooked up as night moved into day, falling asleep in a hazy blue light. About forty-five minutes later, the fire alarm went off in my building. The sun was now completely up and I was suddenly very exposed. It was so loud we couldn't even hear ourselves shout over it. It pounded our intoxicated brains while we motioned to each other and dressed urgently. He rushed around grabbing his things and exited the building without me or my phone number via twenty-four flights of stairs.

Another time I met a Mexican who was ridiculously good-looking but very hard to understand. He got my number and invited me to his place to 'make me dinner'. To his credit, he did actually cook crepes with Nutella for dessert on a single stovetop in the tiny kitchenette of his student accommodation. He then proceeded to feed me like I was a goddess. The romance was very confronting. He kissed me before I had the chance to properly swallow and a Nutella paste still coated my teeth. I was wearing a short skirt and sat awkwardly on his bed, naively trying not to flash my box. He fucked me like the Energiser bunny (not in a good way) and after that night we stayed in contact for a while but it fizzled out.

Casual hook-ups were easier than a relationship for me because I was building my sexual confidence without the added pressure of getting to know someone emotionally and psychologically. I was starting to understand the power between my legs. I was having fun and it was a part of exploring who I was and what I wanted. I kept going this way for a few years after high school, dating on and off. I repeated mantras to myself about the best way to get over someone was to get under someone else, and so on and so forth.

After a while though, I realised I was lonely. Casual flings and short-term meaningless relationships were becoming boring and empty. I slept with a guy who had a girlfriend because it felt risky and exciting, and the next day was fraught with guilt and shame. I felt like a cow giving away my milk for free, and so why would anyone want me? One night I came home at three a.m. after drinking with friends, put on the movie *Closer* and cried myself to sleep. Times were definitely changing.

Physically close yet emotionally far...

Sex can very much intertwine with emotions. It was hard for me to have a one-night-stand without feeling some kind of connection to the other person even if I had no intention of forming a relationship with them. The next day I would find myself hoping that they'd call or wondering what they were doing. It would only last a day or a week at the most but part of me still wanted them to like me even if I didn't like them, or even particularly enjoy having sex with them. This neediness made me annoyed at myself. I craved a partner who understood me and accepted me, and still wanted me regardless of what he found. Intimacy.

I also started to feel frustrated that my casual hook-ups were just sexual servitude. Although I told myself that I was empowered, I never orgasmed from any drunken encounter. My partner would always get what he 'came' for and then afterwards we said our goodbyes. Nowadays I realise this is bad manners but I demanded very little of guys back then. Occasionally sex would trick me into thinking I had romantic feelings but in hindsight I think I was just unsatisfied. Usually when I separated myself from the feelings of lust for that person, I no longer felt anything at all.

The portrayal of sexually-empowered women in the media is becoming more prevalent. Love it or hate it, Sex and the City helped in this regard. It united women of different ages, personality types and values in spreading the acceptance of spreading our legs. However, similar to any other movie or show on television, the characters in this show were just characters and it was a glamorised portrayal of the good, the bad and the ugly within relationships. But at least it got the conversation started.

Sex is a primal desire and isn't shameful or dirty. We are talking about the thing that drives almost every living species on this planet. Without sex, we wouldn't exist. The human race would be doomed. And yet, it is about so much more than procreation and reproduction. The personal connection that you build while you are making love to someone that you trust, and you want them in you and on you, satisfying each other at the same time, and you fall in a sweaty heap together feeling closer than you have ever felt to another human being – then you begin to understand what it is all about. Those early, empty, unsatisfying fucks are just the beginning.

Two consenting adults...

To start experiencing sex like an adult you have to start thinking of it as a responsible self-loving action, like everything else. Sex becomes a part of your self-image, and checking in on your internal world is about being aware of your feelings about yourself and your habitual behaviour. It's all very well to demand your right to be an empowered woman through sex but if you are feeling sad, empty, lonely and unsatisfied on the morning after, then you are not empowering yourself.

Your physical body also needs a mention because it is a big part of discovering your own sexual boundaries. I'm talking safety and disease. It's not all about the fun part, like everything in this world. We'd all like to eat burritos, mud-cake and ice cream with a side of fries for every meal but we know the consequences of that. It's all well and good to desire something, and then get it, like a child would with a treat. But dealing with the consequences of your actions is part of being an adult, doing adult things.

Treating sex with safety in mind is not only for your own physical safety but for the consideration of future partners and even your future children, should you choose to have them. Some sexually transmitted diseases are even cancer-causing, like HPV, or could contribute to later infertility. Yes, condoms are not always one hundred per cent effective but they are more protective than nothing at all.

It's so easy to fall into the trap of hooking up with a guy, getting heavy-handed and wet in all the right places, and realise too late that you have no condom. Then you must make a decision – to root or not to root? These are the different ways it could go:

a) Someone grabs an Uber down to the nearest pharmacy or 7-11;
b) After a quick discussion you decide you both have no diseases and you continue as planned;
c) You feel pressured to continue, and made to feel that by saying no and standing your ground you are denying him his right to fuck you;
d) You say 'no way, Jose' and go to sleep, or satisfy each other in ways that don't involve penetration, or go home.

If you do go ahead with option b) or c), there are more variables. Are you on the Pill? Does he pull out? Did he lie about being recently tested for STIs? The next day you're left questioning if you made the right choice, and know that you really should get the Morning After Pill. Or you wait a few dreadful weeks in the hope that a rush of blood relieves your pregnancy worries. You know you really should make that appointment to get a referral for an STI blood test.

I admit that I've experienced most variables in this scenario and the only one that didn't leave me filled with regret and fear is the one where I just said no and either went to sleep or went home. I didn't always have the guts or sense of control to do that though, if I'm honest with you. There were times when I just wanted the burritos and mud-cake and ice cream and fries.

It's complicated...

Navigating the world of sex is hard enough without further complicating things with disease and pregnancy. Be safe so you can spend your brain power worrying about the normal neurotic things like, "Will they like my body?" "Will my body do what I want it to do?" "Am I too wet, too loose, too hairy, too fumbling?" "Are my nipples weird?" "Does my vagina look like everyone else's?"

The truth is, most guys do not take notice of what vaginas look like. They don't care about your fat roll or the moles on your back. They don't care if your cheeks go red, or your mascara smudges, or your wet vagina 'queefs' (makes a farting noise). Only sociopaths take notice of these things and hold them against you, so if you are being shamed by someone in this way, run fast and far.

Oh, and just in case no one has ever told you, pee after sex. Every time, as soon as possible. All that rubbing around inside your lady parts spreads bacteria around and it is basic hygiene to flush it out. I learned this the hard way. If you don't pee within an hour of having sex, then you might spend the next three days pissing razor blades with a UTI. This is inevitably followed by a round of antibiotics and the joys of thrush due to unbalanced microflora. Some girls I know have never experienced this; however, it is wise not to tempt fate, just get up and pee when you're done.

Sexual Experience and Growth – Reflections

- Your attitude about sex forms a big part of who you are. Explore your own sexuality. What turns you on? How do you feel about your sexual experiences so far? Reflect on what has made you feel good and what hasn't.
- Consider your worst sexual experience, and your best sexual experience. What made them different from each other? What did you learn from each experience?
- Do you enjoy being in relationships and co-learning, or do you prefer a dogmatic approach of figuring out sex with one-night-stands?

- We all have fears when it comes to exposing our true self to others, whether it be physically or emotionally. Consider some of the ways you are scared to be judged, either by your appearance, your sexual ability, or emotional barriers to intimacy.
- Consider how you approach safety when it comes to sex. Is there room for improvement in respecting your body, your partner and your future partners? Think of ways you might work on this, like carrying condoms with you or having stronger boundaries in order to remain aligned with your personal values.

Push it real good...

Sex is the driving force behind almost everything that we know. It helps to sell almost every product on our shelves. It's ingrained within our psyche and shapes our society.

Approach sex with curiosity and accept your own experience level. It's normal to feel terrified, awkward and silly. But at the end of the day, everyone is winging it and every sexual partner is different, so learn what you like instead of feeling like you must please your partner. Take it slow, set your own pace.

Like everything, sex is designed for thorough and mindful exploration. You may not always make good choices. But you're an adult, doing an adult thing, and as long as you take care of yourself and remember that you are in control of what goes in (literally), you'll be okay.

Chapter Eleven
Get Lost and Find Yourself

I love to travel. There's nothing quite like the freedom in getting away from the daily grind, cocktails at eleven a.m., toes in sand, sun on face and the flutter of anticipation in your chest for good times to come. Travel clears your mind, opens your heart with wonder and breaks down your preconceived notions of the world, of the ways in which life should be lived and your self-made personal limitations.

It has been said that travel is the only thing you can buy that makes you richer.

My first overseas holiday was with a girlfriend who is still one of my besties and we went for a two-week trip to Hawaii. We both, coincidentally, happened to be on a 'break' from our respective dysfunctional relationships. We were both unhappy with our boyfriends and the way they treated us but were scared to end it in case we never found love again. My boyfriend knew that we were on a break – I'm not entirely sure that hers did. Regardless, we needed to figure out what we wanted and our holiday was just enough time for our boyfriends to miss us but not move on, and for us to get a ridiculously good tan in the process.

Before we left, I daydreamed about the hot guys I would meet over there, maybe one would like me, maybe we would have a fling. Alas, most of the people we came across were rather fat and obnoxious American tourists or Japanese families, excluding a couple of tanned surfers on the North Shore, whom we admired from afar. I had wrongly assumed that we would spend the two weeks getting over our boyfriends by getting under someone else. It strikes me now how insecure I was that I thought to have a good time, I would need to meet a guy.

After it dawned on us that this wasn't going to be the place where we discovered our Hawaiian soul-mates, we turned to each other instead – and no, not in a lesbian way (although that would be a good story). Our trip ended up being more like two weeks of solid therapy for both of us. We talked, we drank, we danced, we sang, we laughed so hard our stomachs hurt and snorted vodka out of our noses. We smoked cigarettes and discussed our fears, of which there were many. We opened up about our hopes for our lives and our relationships. Having that loving and supportive connection with my friend, combined with fourteen days of good times, was the best medicine I could have asked for during such a messy and confusing time in my life.

We sat on the beach or by the pool each day, roasting in the sun. We took surfing lessons, which challenged both my courage and my co-ordination. We booked an afternoon on a wild party boat with all-inclusive booze, only to realise too late it was actually a romantic sunset cruise. Nonetheless, we ended up best friends with six retired couples by the end of the night. We watched tele-movies on the days we were too hungover to move. When it was time to leave, we cried the whole twelve-hour flight back to Brisbane, listening to sad songs on our iPods and reflecting on photo montages on our digital cameras.

Not all who wander are lost...

Travel changed my reality. Previously I had always spent my time looking inward, thinking about my problems and shortcomings, ignoring the bigger picture. Even though I grew up in a lovely city and was only a short drive from world-class beaches at home, I took it all for granted, as a child would. Taking myself out of my comfort zone and into another part of the world forced me to stop and look around. It made me realise how amazing the world was and how lucky I was to be there to see it. I was able to pause my internal dialogue and just 'be' for a while. The changes that had been brewing within me naturally bubbled to the surface. I was out of my normal routine, so I was forced to take notice of my thoughts and feelings.

I wish I could say that this trip put me in touch with all of the answers and that everything was easy when I got back from Hawaii and had processed my realisations. Of course, it's never that simple. I was still me, and I was still young and confused. I got home and went back to my useless boyfriend (I had *missed* him, after all). I continued on with my job that I thought I loved but actually hated. But something within me had changed. I put it down to the broadening of my perceptions of the world and my place in it. In hindsight, I can see that I was unconsciously put on the path to questioning my understanding of how the world worked. That trip had raised the question, 'What's the point?', and sparked my interest in creating more meaning in my own existence.

Travel Reflections...

- What excites you about travel?
- What scares you about travel? Why?
- If you have travelled before, what did you learn? How did it change you as a person?

I come from a Land Down under...

Since Hawaii, I have seen much more of the world but only a fraction of what I hope to see. Travelling is just something that Australians do. Perhaps because we are geographically isolated from much of the rest of the world, we have an intrinsic insecurity that all of the good action happens elsewhere. And for the same reason, if we are going to bother taking the time and spending the money on airfares, then we are going to make it a hell of a trip and see as much as we can in the time we have. Our close proximity to New Zealand, the Pacific Islands and Asia gives us options for cheap and quick travel destinations, at the same time experiencing culture totally different from our own.

Same, same but different...

When you're advancing out of high school and you continue on with any work or study choices that you've made, even though life has changed a lot, it still consists of many of the same people, the same routines and the same beliefs about yourself. The future feels uncertain even if it's roughly planned out. You're expected to act like an adult but your views of the world are narrow because you simply haven't had the opportunity or disposable income to see, and therefore understand, the world through the eyes of an adult.

That insular mindset can feel so trapping. You know that there's more but you wouldn't have the first clue as to how to connect to it. So you continue on in the same town, doing the same things you've always done, wishing, waiting and wanting more. I spent hours upon hours sitting in my room, listening to emotionally stirring songs about love and friendship, and waiting for the phone to ring and my life to start. Little did I know that life had started whether I was participating or not, even while my thoughts revolved only around myself.

When everything you are doing remains relevant only to the same old people and routines, travel is one way to break free of the constraints of habit.

Travelling forces you to shed all of your ideas of how life is meant to be because suddenly you're surrounded by people who live completely differently from the way that you do, and yet here they are surviving, often thriving but with different ideals and values learned from a life influenced by different culture, beliefs and standard of living. It becomes clear that humanity is more than just seven billion strangers roaming the planet but that, in fact, we are connected to each other through the same spectrum of emotions and desire to live. You realise that life is more than just a series of random events that is happening to you at the centre of it all. Your awareness grows to understand the planet as a buzzing hive of activity, putting your own small life into real perspective.

A major insight which I have learned from seeing the world is that my life is simultaneously meaningful and, at the same time, meaningless. Whilst I'm special and important, there is a greater fabric of activity and meaning that extends beyond my personal existence and into the bigger picture of the rest of the planet. You are unique and exceptional too, and yet you are a tiny speck within our world, within our whole universe, which is full of significance, specialness and uniqueness.

It might seem like a confusing paradox on the surface but for me, this reminder makes me feel like I'm free to disconnect from petty drama and focus on the essence of life which inspires me to do better and be better. If my life is not the centre of the universe, then there's less pressure to get it right and more freedom to experiment in order to find the things that make me happy, and let go of the things that don't. Nothing matters, but I'm also grounded in the fact that everything, and everyone, does.

A whole new world...

Travel gives us a clearer understanding of the world issues that divide us. Some of the differences between cultures and religions are glaringly obvious and occasionally confronting or offensive. We are forced to become clear on our personal version of 'right' and 'wrong', and sometimes completely re-evaluate our sense of justice. However, travel also teaches us the common themes that unite us. When we're born, life drops us into a random circumstance, like a lottery, but we all have the same human instincts which keep us on this planet to make the most of it – survival and love. More often than not, it is easy to find common ground with someone based on the simple joys of life, like food, family and friendship, even when your lifestyles couldn't be more different.

In experiencing a different culture to your own, it naturally brings with it a deep sense of gratitude for what you have back at home. You may also be inspired by the different ways of living life, and take the essence of another culture home with you, like changing your diet or integrating a different work/life balance into your daily routine. You will most certainly find appreciation for sights more divine than you could ever imagine – iridescent blue water, cities and artefacts constructed hundreds or even thousands of years ago, glorious snow-topped mountains and diverse wildlife.

As a society, we have become largely focused on what we can contribute through work, and then gain financially from our career pursuits. When humans were mere cavemen, the working week only consisted of around fifteen hours of hunting, gathering and making things that were necessary for survival and immediate comfort. Stress might be experienced from a lack of food, water or running from a predator, but it would come and go with the seasons, returning to the security of the sense of community within the tribe. There was no shame in relaxing when it was time to relax.

Going on holidays, whether you're driving an hour away from home or getting on a plane for fourteen hours, provides the excuse to sit and just be. You can absorb your surroundings with wonder, rest, reflection and joy. This simple act does more for our sense of self and wellbeing than anything else. This connection with our internal space refreshes our mind and reinvigorates our sense of passion and purpose. If you are a creative soul (or an anxious person who hasn't yet connected with their creative spirit), getting away can shake off brain-drain and mental blockage to rechannel that energy into something positive. It reminds us that we can live our normal lives with less stress and more mindfulness.

We buy into the routine of a forty-hour working week because it's what people do and it's our turn to prove ourselves in the adult world. We want to be taken seriously, dammit. By working hard, and making something of ourselves we'll show everyone – our bosses, our parents and anyone who doubts our worth – that we are successful, and mature and Okay. We continue down this path, and our bosses continue to encourage/push us because they see our potential (and, hey, we're cheap labour at the end of the day). It's difficult to take time off when you're trying to prove your dedication and loyalty in a relatively new career. We bet that we can do that trip better in a couple of years anyway, when we have more time and money.

There'll always be that temptation to put things off into the 'near future', in a few weeks or months, in summer or next year. After the next promotion or when someone else comes back from their holidays. We bet that at this time next year, we'll be in a better position and have the financial resources to buy ourselves our freedom. This mindset is a trap – you are free now. Save what you can, give your boss a month or two's notice, take a week or four off and go on an adventure. *See this world.* You don't even have to spend much money if you can't – take a drive and sleep in the car or a highway motel, or sign up to airline newsletters for cheap flight sales.

Don't wait until retirement to travel – that's forever away, even if you work hard and make enough money to retire while you're still youngish. Besides, what if you never reach retirement? It's not my intention to be morbid but it is a fact that we are all going to die at some point. Once we accept this, we can just get on with it. Fear of death usually comes from the regret of living a life unfulfilled. Make the most of your time on this planet and really live it instead.

Nothing compares to the personal growth that comes from removing yourself from the safety and comfort of your home, routine and loved ones.

We humans are creatures of habit. When you are away from home, you are more likely to try or experience things that you never would in normal daily life. On holidays, you walk around with your eyes open and really take everything in; all of the sights, smells, tastes and sensations of another city or country. You might challenge your fear of heights or the belief that you are not strong or brave enough to do something. You will recognise and stretch your personal limits and remove boundaries that you never even knew you had.

Travel comes with a shit sandwich too…

Don't be disillusioned, though. Of course, it's not all good, all of the time. Long, tedious hours stuck in planes, trains, buses and cars. Gorging on delicious food at every meal seems harmless but does nothing for your waistline or the regularity of your bowel movements. Lugging a suitcase around between cities, too full because you left your home town in winter, and bringing boots with you seemed like a good idea at the time. Awkward miscommunications due to language barriers.

Travelling with friends brings its own challenges when you have different expectations of the trip – sleeping in versus waking up early to sightsee, drinking and partying versus yoga and bushwalks, bungee-jumping versus an art gallery and so on… The practicalities mean that you might come home feeling like you need a holiday from your holiday. Rest assured though, these are the times that you won't remember the most.

Travelling provides a ripe opportunity for self-reflection, whether you like it or not. When you get to where you're going, the shifty shadows of the past and the muddle of emotional trauma that you have been carrying may decide to come with you on your journey. Before you head off, accept that there may be some discomfort in those empty moments between meals, drinks and sightseeing. If you are escaping a rough patch at home, then be mentally and emotionally prepared. Otherwise, it may feel inconvenient, like everything is ruined when you realise your holiday is not necessarily a break from being you.

But it's okay. Say hello to your demons. Tell them they are welcome to join you on your trip. But politely inform them that while they may be freeloading on your generous spirit, they will not be dictating the joy you experience while you are away. But if they are patient, you may have the time and the courage to face things in your downtime. Gently processing these negative thoughts and beliefs will change you as a person, in all of the good ways.

You will still have the best time. Travel provides opportunity for growth in multiple ways. No matter where you go, there you are.

Future Travel Plans...

- What are the top five places you would like to go and why?
- What is one travel goal that you could make happen within the next month? Remember that not all travel has to be expensive, take up a lot of time or even involve leaving the country. Prioritise a new experience.

Chapter Twelve
The Rebellion of Creative Expression

It's easy to think back to my efforts at teenage rebellion – drinking, smoking, staying out late, a lack of respect for my parents and a disdain for how little they knew about Important Things. I fought to be seen as Grown Up. Then, when I turned eighteen, that teenage attitude morphed into camouflaging myself in the adult world. It's funny now to look back and see that my teenage attempts at standing out by being radical and different ended up, only months later, turning into a desperate routine of fitting in through mainstream work and study choices. Keeping within these guidelines, I felt safe, mature and Normal.

I was a particular breed of brat in high school. My siblings and I (there were five of us in our blended family) drove my poor mother to the sharp edge of sanity. Wine was her friend. I'm sure there were many moments where she questioned her life choices. No doubt I owe much of my dogged determination to her – at the end of the day, she had raised me to think for myself. I was a good kid in my heart but definitely tested that theory with my actions. Many were the moments of sullen pouting and sulking because I wasn't allowed to go to a party or hang out aimlessly for days on end at friends' houses.

My mum wasn't super-conservative, she just didn't like the idea of me roaming the streets at all hours of the night with my underage friends. Now that I'm at the ripe old age of Boring, I realise that this is fairly reasonable but at the time I felt like a bird with clipped wings. Desperate not to miss out, I lied often and took advantage of the fact that my mum and stepfather worked long hours to support our family, and weren't always around to keep track of my physical whereabouts.

At eighteen, moving out of home was a continued act of rebellion (and no doubt a relief for my parents). The feeling of freedom was incredible and now I could focus on being Independent. Never mind that Mum still dropped off home-cooked meals to me each week. I went out whenever I wanted, and had boys sleep over without pesky questions about the nature our relationship. I worked weekdays in a suitable job with a vague plan to move up the ladder and have a Career. I moved through the exciting milestones of adulthood and continued repetitively through general life. On and on, day in and day out.

I rationalised that this was what I was meant to do – follow suit and get a job to pay the bills. This was life. It certainly seemed sensible, and I had been raised to be just that. I continued on, mostly sustaining my will to live with getting loose and going out with friends. I held onto delusional dreams of eventual grandeur. There wasn't anything wrong with my life at all. My parents seemed quite satisfied with my choices and I was getting by week to week, paying my rent and buying plenty of snacks. Except that I just felt so… blah. Without really knowing why, my expectations of life were largely unfulfilled.

Checking In…

- What were your expectations of how life should be after school?
- Are you doing the things you thought you would be doing?
- Do you feel the way you thought you would feel?

The calm before the storm...

As we've already discussed, I plodded along like a lost little lamb for years, feeling all of the feelings and not really having any idea what to do with them. I filled my void inside with food, partying and an unhealthy dose of combative drama with my first love. I resisted change and even thinking about what I really wanted. I did whatever I could do to avoid the further discomfort of facing my inner voice. My heart continued to make attempts to communicate with my brain, while I operated in a cloudy haze of fear, self-judgement and denial. Eventually, I could no longer avoid the meltdown and I self-destructed due to a paralysing sense of anxiety and disconnection.

I look back now and see the obvious warning signs – my rigid, inflexible way of thinking about the future, my dogged determination to follow through with the decisions I'd made for fear of appearing childish for admitting I'd made a mistake. I wonder now if all of this confusion and denial might have been avoided if I had had the strength to rebel against society's idea of Adequacy and do my own thing. I realise that this is not a particularly revolutionary thought – these days it seems that every third person is an entrepreneur with some kind of 'start up' business or Instagram mega-profile.

But, this is now and that was back then. No one that I knew personally had ever done anything so radical. My parents had each followed the rules and stayed in their respective jobs or industries for thirty-odd years. I was uneducated about the world and the options that existed. Authenticity was a word that had not reached my vocabulary. These were the days when you still looked for jobs in the Careers section of the newspaper. The internet existed but it wasn't as easily accessible or navigable as it is now. I had no handy blog to refer to for tips and relied solely on the example that had been provided to me.

Mind you, it wasn't a bad example. I followed protocol and got a job – in terms of entry-level, it was a pretty good one, thanks very much. I made my choices for my life and I was determined to persist and follow through with them (however badly it turned out) because I thought that was what grown-ups did. Besides, if I didn't do that, then what would be my alternative? I wasn't open enough to listen to anyone else's advice or consider other options. I stuck to my guns, numbing my instinctual feelings and I blindly continued down the safest road I could find.

Out of touch...

As a young person, I was always a deep thinker. I had always kept journals and diaries and I wrote very heartfelt poetry. In fact, I loved all creative activities until I thought I might not be good at them. I have clear memories of learning to decoupage, linocut and batik. I once was the winner of a drawing competition and my primary school used my drawing as their logo for the school fete. I peaked at about nine or ten years old and then stopped trying because there were others in my class much more naturally talented than I was. It seemed that there wasn't much point in continuing unless you were the best.

My parents did encourage me in their own way but they just aren't gushy people; therefore, I always received fairly lukewarm praise for anything I made or did. They gave me total freedom to be who I was, except I wasn't brave enough to explore how far I could push myself. Also, being creative or artistic made you vulnerable to criticism, and I was not (and still am not) particularly good at swallowing negative feedback.

Looking back, I can see how that creative outlet was helpful for me. I needed all the help I could get figuring things out. I was an anxious and sensitive kid, and keeping a diary was a safe way for me to transfer the noise from my brain onto something that I could read back to myself and decipher in my own time, like hieroglyphics of the heart. Journaling helped me to discover my own point of view. At a time in my life, when emotions ran high and confusion was rife, getting my thoughts down on the page kept me sane.

Putting a pen to paper...

As an adult who was doing all of the respectable things, I was anxious and confused and stressed all of the time. My parents had provided me with a solid example of how to use my head to make logical decisions but somehow I missed the pep talk about the importance of listening to my heart. I wasn't interested in the advice of others anyway, but I was missing the point – I held my own answers and I could have used these same self-therapy tools that I had used in my younger years, like journaling and drawing, to understand myself better and maybe even to have made better decisions.

The greatest act of rebellion is finding your own voice.

As a teenager, I struggled to stand out. As an adult, I fought to fit in. But in the process, I lost sight of who I was. I lost my footing trying to follow an inauthentic path. It took many years for me to reconnect with my creativity and learn how to use it as the tool I needed to connect and become stronger within myself. Only when I reached my late twenties did I wake up to the fact that I needed the process of creation in my life, just as I needed water, vegetables and sunlight. As soon as I made the choice to start writing again, I became grounded in the connection to my inner voice. I remembered who I was. Life became joyful again and I was Okay.

Creative Reflections...

- What are your earliest memories of art/craft/play? What did you love about it or hate about it?
- What are your beliefs about your artistic abilities?
- Did you ever keep a journal? If so, what purpose did it serve? Could that purpose be applicable in your adult life?

Just doing it...

You don't need to be an 'artist'. You don't need to be a 'writer'. You can just be you, and experiment and dabble and try. The more consistent you are, the less pressure there is to do something great. Making creativity a part of your routine each day or week actually gives you more freedom, even though that sounds contradictory. It's about connecting to your spirit, to your voice and to your heart.

I try to write something every day, whether it's free-writing a few pages first thing in the morning or working on a particular project. If I am avoiding a particular project because I am procrastinating or feeling creatively blocked, I might even dabble in other artistic pursuits like oil painting or mandala colouring. Not everything I create is a work of art; in fact, nothing I have made has been worth displaying. For me, I get more out of art than a pretty picture. I become more open to self-expression, and I am able to put a piece of myself on paper or canvas.

Art takes commitment but not seriousness. If I took myself too seriously, then it's likely the perfectionist within me would take over and stop me before I started. So I ignore the fear and self-criticism and create, just for the hell of it. Not so I can sell it, not for people to look at and admire, just because...the idea for this whole book was conceived through my personal need to clean up the mess of feelings and memories from a particularly confusing and consuming time in my life. Sure, I hoped that one day a reader might get something out of it too, but I wrote it for me first.

Looking at art as your meal ticket can suck the fun and the inspiration right out of it. When you have everything riding on your creative projects, you might find that the pressure becomes too much and your creative flow is suddenly stagnant. Art can be a pastime or hobby and not a career and, if that's the case, it's okay.

Keep your day job and come home to your chosen craft at night, knowing that it is sustaining your soul in ways that money never could.

There is no form of artistic pastime that is too corny. Give yourself permission to play and explore. Whether it's building a city of Lego, crafting homemade Christmas cards, crocheting a bikini or making a macramé pot-plant hanger, as long as you enjoy it and it connects you to yourself, that's all that is important. Occasionally, if you are dedicated enough, it may make you money but that should never be the point.

Zoning out...

Art can be a form of meditation too, if it helps to look at it like that. In our world of instant gratification and oversaturation of information, writing and arts and crafts can slow us down just enough to return us to the present moment. The soothing atmosphere and gentle activity allows a sense of focus, whether it's on the movement of the pen on a page, fingers on a keyboard or brush on a canvas. It is simultaneously grounding and centring, and even more so if you can combine the act with exposure to nature. When I can, I choose to write outside, the sounds of birds and crickets or the ocean creating music for my mind.

We don't get this kind of connection to our internal space very often in our lives. When we're alone, we instantly jump on our phones to text or tweet or Snapchat. It's hard to be alone with our thoughts, and even harder to rein in those thoughts to a manageable level. The beauty of being creative is that it enhances our natural state of joy in such a simple and accessible way, by opening up space in our minds and hearts that simply wasn't there before.

Creativity is not a talent that you need to be born with but one you can learn and nurture and continue to grow throughout your life.

There's no time limit or pressure to complete things a certain way. There is no right or wrong, which is precisely the reason why it is both liberating and daunting. There are no instructions, and the outcome is uncertain. This is why you need not be serious about art, because light-heartedness allows your senses to play. Fear hates an uncertain outcome but by creating in the presence of fear, rather than becoming 'fearless', we can learn to create regardless of how vulnerable to judgement or criticism we feel. Putting fear aside when creating teaches us the ability to do this with strength in all areas of our lives.

Permission to play...

The process of play and the connection to your inner child will help you to grow as a person. By giving it more time and attention, you are actually creating a stronger sense of self through exposing your deepest thoughts, feelings and desires. You are connecting to your inner wisdom in order to create the life you want and be the person you want to be. You will be more likely to have answers in confusing and stressful times because you will be able to trust your own gut instincts and decisions.

Having a creative hobby is not just something you put on your resume and can talk about at a job interview. It is an outlet to explore your strengths and weaknesses, your joy and your sadness, and to really get to know the unconscious aspects of your personality. You get to know how you work best; for example, if you are a creative introvert or extrovert. You will know if you are an extrovert by your ability to thrive in teamwork and bounce ideas off others. If you are a creative introvert, it will be obvious by your sheer repulsion of group work and brainstorming, and your desire to think first and explain later. For both personality types, the creative space is the perfect nurturing environment to charge your batteries.

I still get stressed and feel inadequate from time to time (if you are vulnerable, a career in the arts will bring out your best and worst, often at the same time). But never once before have I felt as free as when I am punching keys on my computer, using the same twenty-six letters over and over to create words into sentences, into paragraphs, into narrative. The connection and grounding to my inner world has grown strong, making me feel more gratitude for life, and wonder about this big, crazy world that we live in. No longer do the chains of anxiety shackle me to the insular world of my own petty experiences. And I get all of that out of it, even when ninety-seven per cent of what I write is total shit.

Soul therapy...

Writing and art focuses my anxious, neurotic energy into something a little bit kinder to my soul. My ultimate rebellion as an adult, with my inner child still screaming to be heard, is to buck the normality of the Real World and be who I am on my terms, exploring my mysterious character through words on a page. For you, it might be colours on a page, the meandering loops of yarn for a new scarf or a fragrant floral arrangement. Find the medium that excites you and use it whenever you can. It's a refreshing break from a racing, cynical mind. And cynicism is something that I know a lot about.

I was raised by two cynics, who each came from their respective family of cynics, so you could say that I had somewhat of a sceptical and pessimistic influence on my opinions throughout my formative years. No doubt this was a factor in my rebellious spirit because I questioned everything I was told and considered 'no' as a direct challenge.

These days, I can't watch seventeen seconds of advertising on TV without scoffing and miming that I'm about to heave up my lunch. It makes me a real joy to be around. I constantly question the messages that are a product of marketing, designed to make me feel as if I have a deficit in my life or body that will be satisfied by whatever they are selling. Maybe it's the Taurus in me but I'm like a petulant toddler being spoon-fed pureed apple with my lips shut tight and my arms defiantly placed across my chest. I'm not having any of it.

I feel that becoming more centred through creativity has softened my resolve to prove wrong the societal systems that we are conditioned by. When writing, I am connected to my own spirit and in that moment all of my needs are being met. I am able to let the marketing garbage swirl around me like leaves in the breeze, and I remain peacefully observing the chaos from a safe distance, rather than being dragged into the spiral of disgust and resentment.

I'm grateful for this aspect of my personality – the need to question mainstream opinion and social conditioning fitting us all into a cookie-cutter existence. It feeds into my inquisitive mind and my detached stance on many issues and improves my creativity, just as my creativity conversely softens my hardened edges. Seeing these two separate aspects of my personality blend together makes me appreciate the way I am in a manner that has never been the case.

For a million reasons, suddenly, I am who I was always meant to be.

<u>Integrating creativity into your life...</u>

- List ten of your personality traits, regardless of whether you perceive them as positive or negative (but try to have a blend of both).
- What kind of artistic or creative pursuit would suit your personality? E.g. if you thrive in quiet solitude, or prefer group activities.
- Do you have a part of yourself, or a part of your personal history that could benefit from being expressed creatively?
- How could connecting to your own creativity help you move forward in your own life?

So now, create...

I create. You can too.

It has helped me to respect who I am and what I'm about, for the very first time in my life. I take myself seriously and yet, I am playful. I'm not curing cancer here (or even tinea), but I am listening to my heart, accepting my creative flow, and putting good intention out into the world.

And for me, that's enough.

Chapter Thirteen
Lone Soldier

During the time when I was in high school, being alone forced me into an emotional paradox. It was simultaneously a relief that I could just sit in my room, listen to music and process my feelings of the day's events. But, being alone also made me feel like a loser with no friends. I imagined everyone else doing fun things together after school and on the weekends that I either wasn't invited to or wasn't allowed to go to.

Being alone exposed all of my self-esteem issues and gave me exponentially greater opportunities to sit and think about all the ways I wasn't good enough.

When I was alone, I was lonely. Simple as that. I had no concept of keeping myself company, as a friend might when you hang out one-on-one. I craved human connection and someone who might really listen and truly understand me, but I was also shy and found it difficult to be myself around others. I wanted love. At that time in my life, love meant approval from friends or from boys and when I didn't get it, it led only to further loneliness and pain. By projecting my emotional needs onto other people, I was relying on my friends to fill a void that they simply could not fill. I lacked the ability to love, support and nurture myself.

After high school, when some of that emotional turmoil settled down a bit, things weren't as bad but I still felt lonely in my own company. 'Unfulfilled' was my middle name. My friendships were pretty shallow at that time and I had only experienced meaningless romantic relationships. I knew I was feeling things too deeply, that things weren't as they should be, and I was missing an important piece of the puzzle. But without the emotional maturity to look inwards, I remained bitterly disappointed when the people in my life failed to lift me up and make me feel Normal.

The feeling of missing out on something important extended to jealousy and resentment of my friends, and brought up paranoid suspicions of them doing fun things without me. If I didn't hear from my friends, I automatically assumed that no one liked me and everyone was laughing about me behind my back. No doubt I was probably a bit difficult to be around. I was needy but I didn't act needy. I couldn't openly admit that I was struggling. Instead, I built an impenetrable wall to protect my vulnerable self.

When I was able to let my guard down, I knew I had strengths that I brought to the table. I was fun. I was a good friend who took a genuine interest in and care for my friends' lives. My self-loathing and lack of confidence just got in the way. I was just too raw at times, causing my friends to feel uncomfortable and they had neither the inclination nor the skills to support me. I had a lot of demons that I was scared of facing, and they were each busy dealing with their own as well.

Checking In…

Solitude

- What does that word mean to you?
- Does it bring up feelings of boredom or loneliness? Does it make you feel nervous? Does it make you feel relieved, like you can finally be yourself and stop pretending?

The road to realisation...

With my special ability to do everything the absolute hardest way, it took years of relearning and reconnecting to who I was before I was able to let go of my insecurities and improve my relationship with myself.

Most of my self-discovery stemmed from the times I was feeling hard-done-by in my friendships or relationships because I didn't feel I could rely on others to really be there for me. I didn't realise at the time but I was lumping the people in my life with the task of improving my self-esteem, which simply wasn't part of their job description. I didn't have the backbone for confrontation so when I felt resentful, I forced myself into isolation to wallow in my misery.

Wallowing didn't feel good (in fact, it was downright depressing) but it did provide me the opportunity for reflecting upon what was really going on and how much of my heartache was caused by my own actions. I eventually called myself out on my own emotional bullshit and could gain understanding of how I invited or blocked the kinds of people I wanted in my life. I even grew to appreciate my own company after a while.

Quiet time...

Being alone brings up all of the things we are trying to quash. Rarely are we ever truly alone, reaching for our phone or the TV remote to make external noise in our ears and our minds, blocking any internal vibrations that might be suggesting something important. We humans are complex beings – without the time and space to decompress and process our emotional and psychological Stuff, we end up feeling overwhelmed and burnt out. Being alone and making a conscious decision to be, puts us in a position to separate the white noise from significant intuitive clues.

Solitude Reflections...

- Think of the last time you were alone. Did you feel uncomfortable and automatically reach for your phone or turn on the television?

In motion...

I often get caught up in my own head. If you are like me, you might spend too much time making lists, considering pros and cons, and getting paralysed with indecision. Others get caught up in the heart, being led through life by feelings. Thoughts and emotions roll in and out of our conscious mind and body, all day, every day.

When I am thinking a negative thought, it is usually accompanied by a negative feeling. I like to remember the actual word 'emotion' and liken it to its root 'motion', which accurately indicates how we all fluctuate at some measure of the emotional scale at all times. A feeling, or the thought in which it stems from, does not need to dictate my day or what I believe to be true about myself, especially when it might be very different, in a minute, an hour, a day, a week or a year.

We are social creatures...

We each express our social tendencies in different ways, depending on personality but most of us impulsively seek regular human connection of some description.

Are you an introvert or extrovert? I'm personally a pretty even mix of both. I definitely need alone time to recharge my batteries but if I spend too much time alone, I go stir-crazy and need to be around people. If you are introverted, it's likely that you already spend time alone to chill out and refuel your resources. It's important that you make the distinction between just being alone and consciously connecting with your inner space. Extroverts may thrive in the company of others but it is just as important that they take time in their own skin for grounding and avoid using the need to be around others as a distraction technique from connecting with their internal being.

Layers of the conscious mind...

Our conscious mind can drone on continuously with thoughts and feelings and judgements throughout our day. We dwell on past experiences and worry about possible future experiences, dreading the worst case scenario. If you sit and listen for a minute to the rattling of your own conscious mind, it becomes quieter and you find that there is a deeper observation that occurs from another layer of the mind. Eckhart Tolle calls this the Silent Observer, in his book *The Power of Now*. The Silent Observer is the watcher of the conscious mind, taking note of everything going on and patiently waiting for the opportunity to give the conscious mind a rest through mindfulness.

The conscious mind that produces our thoughts and feelings can be monitored and controlled by our Silent Observer. The Observer in us might be our soul, our inner voice, our subconscious mind or whatever other commonly-named entity that you wish to liken it to. The Observer is always there, and being present in the moment through mindfulness allows it to take over. Meditation is one way to let the conscious mind stop and rest and breathe by being truly present with the Observer.

This may all sound a bit weird if you have no experience with mindfulness or meditation. Keep in mind that 'mindfulness' just means 'presence'. I have to admit that my own relationship with meditation has been non-committal. When I do take the time though, I'm calmer and my emotions are more stable. I trust myself more. There are other ways I might get this same connection to my inner self with techniques that are similar to a meditative state.

I'm always willing to try anything that draws me out of my mind, constantly filled with neurotic thoughts, and into the present moment where I can peacefully connect on a deeper level with what's going on around me and what's going on within me.

Pressing pause and being mindful at least once per day gives us the opportunity to be free of influences like our own self-judgement and the opinions of others in order to fully connect into our true spirit. This might bring up some internal questions or expose some fears you have been unconsciously letting dictate your actions in life. Mindfulness gives us the chance to accept all of those parts of ourselves without further condemnation but love and support, and makes it easier to define what we want while growing into more fulfilled, compassionate and aligned human beings.

Activities of the Lone Soldier...

If meditation is not your thing, there are lots of ways to connect into a mindful state of being. It might be as simple as sitting on a park bench and listening to the birds. I write. Or paint. I sit in nature and watch the clouds and the trees. I play with or cuddle my two cats. I read a book. I could do a work-out, or yoga or go for a walk around the block or a swim in the ocean. I do anything to switch the noise-setting on my conscious thoughts to silent so that I can be present and see what comes up for me, physically, emotionally and psychologically.

Remember that there is no right and wrong in observing your own conscious mind. It sounds simple enough but it is quite challenging when you are learning how. The point is to practise until it becomes natural to give your full attention to your inner and outer life, and drown out the constant drone of meaningless thoughts, opinions and judgements about yourself and others. Be compassionate to yourself – there is no point in berating yourself for thinking negatively. We all do it. Approach this exercise with curiosity, awareness and self-acceptance.

Reflections

List five things that you enjoy doing that bring you into the present moment, where you might consciously look around and absorb your surroundings fully and openly. Think of the ways in which you can incorporate these more often in your life.

Out of the mind and into the body...

Dealing with the issues that appear when you're alone is crucial, not only for your state of mind but for your physical health. Being present gives you the opportunity to be able to check in with your physical body and intuitively know when something isn't right. For instance, you might check in and realise how tired and tense you are, or how your digestion is not quite right. Experiencing consistent feelings of loneliness, jealousy and resentment has scientifically shown to have detrimental effects on the body, like the physical effects of stress, chronic inflammation and gastro-intestinal problems, and can possibly lead to anxiety and depression.

If you can learn to exercise your ability to be alone without feeling lonely or isolated, just like you would with any other muscle in your body, then you are going to be more resilient and have a healthier, happier life. You will strengthen your relationship with yourself and learn to be your own best friend. You will become kinder to yourself, accepting of your vulnerability and therefore a stronger person.

Being in control of your own 'stuff'...

I believe we are all the masters of our own destiny if we have the courage to face what that really means. We all need support in our lives but ultimately it is up to us to take control of our shit and do something with the short stint we have been allocated in this life. It might feel like you have time to fuck around, but you don't. No one is going to save us from ourselves. They're too busy dealing with their own stuff. Likewise, if you are trying to save someone else from their life, it's likely that you will drown whilst trying to be their raft.

The flow-on effects from listening to yourself and trusting yourself are huge. You build a positive relationship with yourself and are therefore able to look after yourself better and create stronger boundaries with the people in your life. This means that you can be a stronger pillar of support without getting drawn into the emotional turmoil or drama of friends and family. It puts everything in perspective. Will this thing you are stressing about right now matter in a year's time? What about a week's time? The frame of the window in which you view your world widens and your outlook on the future changes.

A deeper meaning, a bigger picture...

I have always been one of those annoying people that seeks meaning in life and every experience and thing within it. My journey of self-reflection has always been a spiritual one, even as a child. I can't look up at the sky without wondering, "What does it all mean?" I imagine how small I am, and how my personal existence is just one tiny piece of an unfathomable puzzle.

Though I've never been particularly religious, connecting to myself has also given me a sense of connection to something bigger, stronger and more powerful than my human brain can understand. By learning to trust myself, I have gained trust in the universe and some kind of larger master plan, of which I need not know all of the details. While I'm still exploring my beliefs, I find it enriching to pass over some of the responsibility to something greater than myself. Things can pan out the way they must, and I can stop sweating the small stuff. That leaves me more time to focus on the things that feel important – truly living, loving and creating.

So, go within. Be brave enough to seek the answers that lie within you. Be brave enough to trust yourself. You are everything you were meant to be – a perfect mess of a human being.

Ten-Minute Mindfulness Meditation

Sit comfortably on the floor or on a chair, or lie down if you prefer. Set your phone to silent and set an alarm for ten minutes (this will put an end time on it and ensure you stay as present as possible for ten minutes).

Start to become conscious of your breathing. Connect to your internal rhythm and slow it right down so that each breath in lasts for a count of five seconds, and each breath out lasts for a count of five seconds. Remain this way for about ten to fifteen breaths.

Become consciously aware of your physical body. Feel your way through any parts of your body with tension, pain or uneasy feelings. Start with the top of your head and consciously move down through your body to the tips of your toes. Tense and relax any sore or tight spots as you go.

Check in with your thoughts. Are they clear or are they racing? Use your Silent Observer to notice the thoughts that creep into your conscious mind. Imagine that they are clouds floating by. There is no need to pay them great attention, just allow them to pass.

Consider any emotions that rise up to the surface. Feel your way into them to see if there are deeper emotions needing to be expressed. Discover what lies at the core of your irritation, your sadness, your anger, your tiredness. Spend as much time as you can allowing thoughts and feelings to be heard, accepted and let go.

Continue breathing slowly. When you feel intuitively ready to finish, gently wriggle your fingers and your toes, coming back into the present moment. Slowly open your eyes, gather your thoughts and go forth in your day. Take note of anything in a journal that came up for you that might be worth consciously working on further.

Conclusion

I wish I could wrap up the process of personal growth into a neat, pretty little package. The reality is that I can't. The years of high school and beyond are an ugly, awkward, messy time of flailing and finding your feet. It's a cross-country road trip without Google Maps, and it's a different origin and destination for every woman in this world.

The only thing you can do is throw yourself into entirely new experiences to see what fits and see what feels like shit. Working, studying, living away from home, making new friends, losing old ones, falling in love and building your relationship with yourself will bring out every strength and every weakness that you have learned or been conditioned with throughout your life.

You will likely fuck up and make bad decisions. You will test every personal boundary and ethical standard that you hold dear for the sake of love, or to impress someone, or to make yourself feel good. But that's Okay.

Remember that there is only one of you on this planet. You are here for a reason, and you possess unique gifts and experiences that no one else has. You have no competition. A life of comparison will bring you undoubted misery, so accept your circumstances of random selection and get on with it. There's no more time to waste.

No longer a child, or a victim, you are in control of what happens next.

Let go of your bitterness and resentment towards all of the people who have wronged you – these emotions are not helping you to grow. Conversely, they will tear you into parts as you are scrambling to become whole. There is an entire life to be lived and it has already begun. You are far too intelligent and thoughtful to be squandered as another tortured soul on this Earth. There are already too many of those on the downward spiral to mediocrity, to alcoholism and to depression.

It's quite a wondrous opportunity that we are given to experience the human existence as who we are. Who knows why we are chosen to live our lives, but don't you dare waste it. Play, laugh, create, connect and truly do what brings you happiness. Don't rely on Instagram quotes to do this for you, make it happen on the inside. The magic you hold inside will materialise when you are emotionally mature and resilient enough to be grounded in your true self, raw in your talents and vulnerability, and take what comes in your life with dignity, gratitude and strength.

Be a strong woman, even if you haven't been shown how. Be cautious and smart enough to understand the agenda of others but brave enough to let love in. You might get hurt but you can take it. You're tougher than you give yourself credit for.

Learn to fill up yourself with love first, before you give it away. Otherwise you risk setting yourself up for a lonely life of dependency, on people or on substances. Define what you want and stay open to this changing over time. Focus on how you want to feel, and the rest will come.

See the world. It's not that big but the surprises are endless. Travel gives you the excuse to get out of your comfort zone and stretch your imagination to new possibilities. When you learn to go inward, you also learn to start looking outward to the experiences of others. Be a beacon for others who are struggling and influence them to be stronger within themselves. Your encouraging energy will attract more positive people and things into your life.

Make the choice to be happy now, as much as you can. Savour life and do more of the things that satisfy you and make you feel content. Continue to connect with your whole self and with real joy as often as possible.

Most importantly, get to know who you are – she is worth getting to know! Like her. Love her. Trust her. Look upon her as your closest friend and ally. Because, at the end of the day, she is.